Alan Lucas was born and raised in Belfast during the troubles, and wondered from a young age why people would kill others just because they had developed different beliefs.

He studied for a lightweight degree in Leisure Studies, a Master's degree in more of the same and graduated as a top student of leisure while spending most of the time skiing.

After university, he worked as a ski teacher in the U.S., New Zealand, Australia and Europe. He had proper jobs as a marketing boss at global sportswear brands Nike and Adidas and has founded various businesses.

As an entrepreneur, coach and motivational speaker, Alan is passionate about self-improvement and helping people have more fun and fulfilling lives. He created the Sort Your Self Out system, and the EGO HERE brand which donates much of its profits to the SYSO Foundation, providing personal development resources for young people to help them avoid becoming messed-up older people.

youdontneedtherapy.com

You Don't Need Therapy

Alan Lucas

Published by Beak Street Publishing 2021

Copyright © 2021

First edition.

The author asserts the moral right under the Copyright, Designs and Patents Act 1988 to be identified as the author of this work.

All rights reserved. No part of this publication may be reproduced, stored in a retrieval system or transmitted, in any form or by any means without the prior consent of the author, nor be otherwise circulated in any form of binding or cover other than that with which it is published and without a similar condition being imposed on the subsequent purchaser.

ISBN: 978-1-913532-25-3

Also available as an ebook
ISBN: 978-1-913532-26-0

Printed by Clays

Disclaimer

The information in this book is designed to provide ideas on how to think differently about life. Any opinions and suggestions by the author are merely that, and the author and publisher offer no warranties or guarantees for any of the content or how it is applied. You are responsible for your own choices, actions and results.

Although the author and publisher have made every effort to ensure all information in this book was correct at the time of going to press, the author and publisher do not assume and hereby disclaim any liability to any party for any loss, damage or disruption caused by errors or omissions, whether such errors or omissions result from negligence, accident or any other cause.

None of the material in this book is meant to be used, nor should be used, to diagnose or treat any medical condition. The book is not intended as a substitute for the medical advice of doctors and the reader should consult their medical practitioner for advice in relation to any suspected medical condition.

"The helping hand you need can usually be found at the end of your own arm." – Irish proverb

The SYSO System®

Sort Your Self Out

People are seeking help for mental health problems at an unprecedented rate. In the UK, one in four report experiencing mental health issues and one in eight are receiving some form of prescribed 'treatment'. Life should be better than ever, but we describe ourselves as being more messed up than ever, and it's a worldwide problem.

According to the World Health Organisation there is a suicide every 40 seconds. In the UK alone, 16 people choose to end their lives every day, and tragically this is the biggest cause of death for under 35s. We have a chronic mental health problem. Medication and therapy, the conventional default solutions, are expensive and don't seem to be working. Antidepressant sales are running at $15 billion a year, yet some studies suggest people taking antidepressants are 2.5 times more likely to kill themselves. In the UK 1.4 million people were 'prescribed' therapy on the NHS last year and a lot more are waiting on long lists for appointments. The costs are escalating, yet our mental wellbeing is worse than ever.

Drugs and talking are not the answers; having a clear, easy-to-follow system to sort your shit out, and taking action, is. You don't need therapy; you can sort your self out when you know how.

A huge number of people are reaching out for help with their mental health but there are also many who want help but don't feel comfortable asking, or who find it confusing or overwhelming to know where to start and what to do. The resources available are plentiful but can be hard to access, seem gimmicky, or the solutions are simply ineffective. There are over 160 recognised types of psychotherapy, and endless counselling styles, coaching methods, healing techniques, retreats, seminars and book offerings. The language used can be daunting and jargonistic, but people don't care about the labels and terminology, they just want solutions and results. They aren't broken, they don't need 'treatment', they just need an easy-to-follow system to sort themselves out and they need to take action. Clarity and taking effective action are the keys to making your life better, whereas talking therapies and medication can keep people in their problems longer than necessary.

Change can happen quickly when you know how, and if you follow the principles of the 7-Step Sort Your Self Out (SYSO) System, you'll change how you think, which will change how you feel, which will change what you do, all as quickly as you choose. Changing your life isn't that complicated when you know how, and when you know how, you don't need therapy.

The SYSO System is a practical 7-Step system that anyone can apply to change their life. The system cuts through the deep forest of existing self-help material by distilling into a universal solution, 7 principles which can be applied wherever you are on your journey. Self-help and self-development material is often unnecessarily overcomplicated and heavy, but the SYSO System is a straightforward, action-based approach to changing your life, and this book is filled with exercises so you can DO the changing, rather than just read about it. The system challenges conventional wisdom in areas like mind management, emotions and purpose, and introduces – amongst many other ideas – a new concept, 'usefulment' – the feeling of being fulfilled by being useful.

As chronic as our mental health issues are, with effective solutions changes can happen quickly and we will come to realise that most of the crap we feel in our lives is of our own making. We're increasingly understanding that we have perhaps been looking in the wrong places and in the wrong ways in our pursuit of happiness, and encouragingly more and more people are questioning their lives and instead seeking wisdom, authenticity, simplicity and spiritual awakening as they strive for a more fulfilling experience.

"If you want things to change, you have to change." – Jim Rohn

Introduction

"I think everybody should get rich and famous and do everything they ever dreamed of so they can see that it's not the answer." – Jim Carrey

As I waited for my client to arrive, I looked out over the London skyline from the panoramic windows of the unnecessarily fancy meeting room. The city appeared full with so many buildings, old and new, packed in tightly, with many more pushing upwards in various stages of construction. I wondered if the city would have also seemed full back in 1311 when St Paul's Cathedral was the tallest building in the world or in 1895 when London was the largest city?

Half a century ago there were only two cities in the world with more than 10 million people. Today there are almost 50, with London now considered relatively small as megacities have developed with populations of over 30 million. Throughout the world, humans are choosing to live closer to each other than ever before. Three hundred years ago, 2% of the world's population lived in urban areas; now that figure is over 50%. Innovation in engineering, construction and technology are making this possible, as we build higher and deeper, creating denser urban environments to call home.

Down at ground level, people the size of ants were moving through the labyrinth of streets overshadowed by enormous buildings. It is remarkable that humans, so physically small in comparison to their environment, could collectively build such giant and complex urban areas with all the logistical, engineering, building and management challenges. One person on their own can only do so much but as a race we have made phenomenal advancements and created so much that was previously unthinkable, by working together.

In the sky, I could see the flight path of just a few of the thousands of planes that are in the airspace above London every day. Humans have designed ways not only to fly like birds but to do so in such comfort. Flying through the sky to faraway lands would have likely seemed unimaginable to our not too distant relatives, yet here we are on the verge of commercial space travel and heading towards what Elon Musk describes as becoming a "spacefaring civilisation and multiplanetary species." We really have achieved things that are literally out of this world already, and this may just be the beginning.

Innovation continues apace. The inventor and futurist Raymond Kurzweil describes The Law of Accelerating Returns, where the rate of change in a wide variety of technologies tends to increase exponentially. Because of these accelerating returns of converging technologies, Kurzweil, using mathematical modelling, predicts we're going to experience the equivalent of 20,000 years of technological innovation over the next 100 years. Already things that seemed just fantasy are very real such as driverless cars, robots, virtual reality and artificial intelligence, and planning is well under way for superfast transportation using magnetic levitation. It's only 50 years since the internet was created, and more recently mobile phones, yet we take these technologies for granted already. What will we take for granted in another 50 years? It certainly seems likely that "The future is faster than you think" as Peter Diamandis and Steven Kotler outline in their great book of that name.

Congratulations to humans! If we were receiving our latest school report, it might suggest we're doing brilliantly:

"Well done humans. Innovating and achieving to the highest standard. Great progress. A fantastic performance and a very exciting future ahead."

But this isn't the whole story, is it? There's much more to our overall schooling and human experience than all these fantastic achievements. How well have we been looking after our home, Planet Earth? How are we doing looking after ourselves, physically and emotionally? Are we living happily together with love and understanding? Are the lives we have full of joy, and rich in meaning? Are we clear in our belief about why we are here? Are we taking responsibility for our experience of living?

If our school report was issued for our performance in these areas, unfortunately it would be very disappointing; the school would be calling in our parents!

"Damaging their home. Needs urgent attention. Mostly in a very poor general physical state. Often unable to get on well with others who have different views. Failing to take responsibility for how they feel and not realising their human potential. Overall most seem a little lost and somewhat self-obsessed. Significant work to be done. Big concerns about the future of these students and those that follow."

With all the innovation and achievements we have made, the core measure for the quality of our human experience is really how fulfilled we feel, and in that we are falling short. We have achieved so much that is remarkable but we seem perhaps to have lost our way a little, as if we have been missing the important goals while chasing those we thought would bring untold happiness. There are many studies that show in spite of all the progress we are making in the developed world, the bottom line is that we are unhappier than ever, and alarmingly it is often especially our children who are reporting the most unhappiness despite living at a time when there is more opportunity than ever. Of course we want to experience and push for all the exciting innovations humans are capable of, but we need to ensure we are happy, fulfilled, and getting along with each other or all the amazing technological advancement will seem inconsequential.

We haven't looked after the place we live very well and the damage to our home, Planet Earth, is now revealing itself beyond doubt. Our destruction of biodiversity and the ecosystem has reached levels that threaten our wellbeing. We see climate change in weather patterns, across farmland, throughout plant and animal habitats. We are using up finite natural resources at an alarming rate, and we are destroying our water supply with toxic chemicals, damaging the most valuable resource our planet has to offer. We even have a garbage island floating in our ocean, mostly comprised of plastics, the size of India, Europe and Mexico combined.

Most people are also trashing their bodies, the vehicle in which they journey through life. According to the World Health Organization, around 31% of adults aged 15 and over are too inactive with approximately 3.2 million deaths each year attributable to insufficient physical activity. Read that again – 3.2 million people dying each year because they don't move enough! This is insanity! I used to work as a marketing executive at Nike where we ran the very successful and simple call to action marketing slogan, *Just Do It!* When I read the statistics on how people are deciding to be inactive I felt like the government should start a *Just Fucking Move!* campaign.

What we put in our mouths is also making us seriously sick, and The Office for National Statistics reports 29% of adults in England are obese with a further 36% unhealthily overweight. Obesity in childhood is especially alarming and is associated with a wide range of serious health complications. An estimated 2 million people in the UK are also living with a diagnosed food allergy and the UK has some of the highest rates of allergic conditions in the world. We urgently need to sort our bodies out and to do this we need to move more, eat more healthily and live in a less chemically polluted environment.

We're also not in great shape mentally. We face an epidemic of addictions, and reports of unhappiness are off the scale. The number of people who self-harm or have suicidal thoughts is drastically increasing. Whether anxiety, depression, phobias, obsessive compulsions or the ridiculously labelled 'low mood disorder', our mental health needs urgent attention.

Humans have made incredible jaw-dropping buildings, aeroplanes and computers, we have sent people to space, made phenomenal advancements in medicine, technology, engineering, science and entertainment and created new ways of pleasuring ourselves, but we are trashing our planet, our bodies and our minds. Our school report in these areas is chronic and demands we make changes immediately.

The good news is that as students of life, we can. We just need to know what to do. Our brains are capable of creating the remarkable, there's no doubt about that, but our brains operate by taking directions and it is time to check that the directions we're giving are taking us to the outcomes we want, and to the lives full of joy and passion we are capable of experiencing. It all starts with our mind and our inner world and if we sort ourselves out on the inside first, we'll make better choices, and make a better life for ourselves and future generations, while magnifying the enjoyment of all the technological advancements and converging technologies coming our way. It all starts with developing ourselves.

"Hi, I'm Alan, great to meet you," I said, putting my hand out to greet Anne as I opened the meeting room door.

"I'm Anne. My life is a total mess," she told me. "It's going to take a lot of sessions to help me. I'm so broken I don't know if you'll be able fix me."

As a coach, it is common to hear clients using language in this way, but Anne had delivered her self-diagnosis and conclusions before even sitting down. This was not the greeting and preamble that usually begins each coaching session. I asked Anne first to take a seat, suggested she have a drink of water, and do some simple deep breathing exercises until she felt relaxed and calmer, as much as someone who thinks their life is a total shambles can be!

"What makes your life a total mess?" I asked. "I've been through hell," replied Anne. "I have had so much to deal with I don't even know where to start. My life has been dreadful, nobody deserves what has happened to me. I often wonder if my life is worth living."

Most problems of the mind, and our experience of life, are to do with how we look at things and how we talk to ourselves and Anne was giving an excellent example of how to look at things and talk to yourself in a way that is guaranteed to make you feel shit.

"So, what would you like your life to be like?" I asked, but Anne continued ranting and waffling on again about what was wrong. She was focusing on what she didn't like, and was telling herself how bad her life was. This was making her feel even worse. She was feeding her mind programmes to feel bad, rather than focusing on what she did want and feeding her mind programmes to feel good. What we tell our brains is what they'll believe. It isn't that complicated.

"My life is broken. I have so much crap going on. I'm a total basket case," Anne wailed, adding intense emotion to her already unhelpful thoughts. Anne was, of course, doing what many people who don't feel great about their lives do. Life hadn't worked out the way Anne had thought it should, so she was looking at things in an unhelpful way and telling herself she was a mess, and that she couldn't change how she felt about her life.

She had assumed some form of therapy was the answer. Anne had definitely felt pain, as we all do and will at times, and for this I felt sympathy, but what if Anne could see that everything in her life so far was preparing her with invaluable tools for the next part? What if Anne realised she had everything she needed *inside her* to make an outstanding life full of joy and fulfilment? What if she decided now, this moment, to take responsibility for her experience of life? What if she realised no matter what happened outside which she couldn't control, she could always control her feelings inside? What if she awoke to the realisation that deep in her soul she was an unlimited fountain of love and strength and that she just needed to uncover and unleash who she really was?

Without going into the specific detail of Anne's particular case, and the outcome she achieved by following the simple and clear principles of the 7-Step SYSO System, it was this interaction with Anne that made me want to write this book. I actually worked with lots of Annes and saw clients from all walks of life who had sought help making changes. Sometimes they didn't know what they wanted, or they were struggling with emotional pain, anxiety and depressive thinking, or sometimes their life was going well in some areas but they wanted to grow and be more. The common denominator was that every person had contacted me believing they needed professional help and likely lots of it in the form of one-to-one sessions.

Around the time I met Anne it was already becoming a challenge to fit in clients for repeat bookings or to accommodate recommendations, and I had already been wondering about other ways to help more people but in a more time-efficient way. I was also, in all honesty, getting frustrated listening all day to people talking about their problems! As much as I enjoyed helping people, it felt like the same old stuff over and over again, as most people's problems arise from the same basic core issues.

I was also becoming more aware and somewhat surprised at just how many people considered their lives to be at least a bit fucked up and were struggling emotionally, and just how few people were really loving their lives! Of course, I was seeing the ones who considered themselves really messed up, but in my nonprofessional everyday life I was not seeing many people overflowing with joy, living authentically with an appreciation for the gift that is their life.

Anne, like all the clients I saw, was not seriously mentally unwell, but rather just needed to know what to do to change and then she needed to activate herself to do it. I knew that Anne didn't need to spend lots of money on many sessions with me, or anyone else; the process I was going to run through with her was a series of 7 Steps which she could easily do on her own in her own time at her own pace. She just needed to know what to do and then have exercises to activate the doing.

After my meeting with Anne, I decided to put the 7-Step SYSO programme into a book, accessible to everyone for the price of a good pizza, rather than people thinking they needed to spend hundreds or thousands of pounds on therapy, retreats, gurus or seminars.

So here it is.

If you would like to make changes to your life, read the book, and do what it says. The system is simple. 7 chapters. 7 Steps. You will learn how to expand your awareness, become a great manager of your mind, take charge of your emotions, meet your needs in healthy ways, have a crystal-clear philosophy for the purpose of your life, understand that everything is interconnected, and how to make your life more enjoyable by enhancing the lives of others. You will light up and lighten up, leading more from your heart than your ego, being focused on feeling fulfilled by being useful.

By following the Steps, you will change the filter through which you experience life and by changing the filter, everything will look different. You will have a new perspective, clarity of purpose and your life should feel amazing and exciting. The sum of the steps is greater than the parts, each step amplifying the others, and you can revisit any part at any time to really engrain your learning.

The system includes lots of exercises to help you make the changes to your life, rather than just reading about them. They are simple and mostly quick to do, requiring little more than in some cases a pen and paper or note making on your phone or computer. Practise these exercises as often as you like. To have an excellent life, like training to be excellent at anything, involves regular practise and developing helpful habits. Making an outstanding life isn't a single event, it is an ongoing journey of growth and development.

You Don't Need Therapy challenges people to think differently about how to change, and before I get criticised by many people who will have benefitted enormously by various types of therapy or coaching, to be clear I am absolutely not saying therapy is not useful in certain situations. I know there are many wonderful therapists, counsellors and coaches who work tirelessly to help others and who should be applauded. However, in my view, most people don't need to spend lots of money to sit through lots of sessions in a strange meeting room talking over and over about their past and their problems. They just need to know what to do to change and then they need to take action, and the SYSO System provides these tools and at a fraction of the price of even a single therapy session. Surely that's at least worth a try if you are considering therapy, or are 'in therapy' and aren't getting the results you want?

Often we know what to do, but we stumble with the doing, and the SYSO System covers how to unblock yourself if you're stuck. Sometimes we feel lost and aren't sure of our reasons, and the SYSO System will help you answer these and the bigger questions that lie behind how you live. And sometimes we can feel our life is on fire, that we are living from our hearts and everything is great. If that's you, the SYSO System can help you keep growing, do more and share your gifts.

Constructing skyscrapers, sending people to space, and creating robots are difficult tasks, but changing how you look at things and what you say to yourself really isn't. We just haven't been taught how to do this very well. All the tools you need are distilled in this book and you now have the springboard to change your life as much as you choose, and quickly. Wherever you are on your journey, your life can be more, and if you lead with heart, it really isn't that complicated.

You don't need therapy!

STEP 1
Become More Aware

"When you go out into the woods, and you look at trees, you see all these different trees. And some of them are bent, and some of them are straight, and some of them are evergreens, and some of them are whatever. And you look at the tree and you allow it. You see why it is the way it is. You sort of understand that it didn't get enough light, and so it turned that way. And you don't get all emotional about it. You just allow it. You appreciate the tree. The minute you get near humans, you lose all that. And you are constantly saying 'You are too this, or I'm too this.' That judgment mind comes in. And so I practice turning people into trees. Which means appreciating them just the way they are." – *Ram Dass*

There are approximately 7.7 billion people on this planet today, and each year new arrivals, less departures, brings a net addition of around 80 million. However, those of us currently living represent only about 7% of the total number of humans who have ever lived. Since modern Homo sapiens first walked the earth around 50,000 years ago, more than 108 billion members of our species have existed. Altogether, dead and alive, that is a lot of human life!

The actual numbers can be hard to put in perspective at that scale. Think of the largest number of people you have ever seen together at any time, either in person at an event, in photographs or even in film.

If you've been to a large stadium, to see a concert or sports event, it probably felt like you were amongst a huge number of people, especially when you tried to leave. Yet even the larger venues in the world, such as the Michigan Stadium (capacity 107,000), the Melbourne Cricket Ground (100,000) or Twickenham Rugby Stadium (82,000) can hold only a relatively tiny number of people.

Massive music festivals like Glastonbury or Coachella host around 200,000 and 120,000 people respectively, and occasionally there are huge, one-off religious festivals or celebrations that involve hundreds of thousands to even a few million. But, even if you were at one of these events or have seen images of the crowds or can visualise the scale of these sorts of gatherings, the numbers still represent only a tiny fraction of the number of people alive right now, today, on Planet Earth, and an even tinier fraction of all the human beings who have ever lived.

You are unique

The number of human beings that have been created is remarkable, but even more so is that every single one, wherever and whenever they have lived, is a different expression. All unique expressions of life and all evolving differently. So, 108 billion different versions of people have been produced so far in the story of human life, and no two are the same. It's a fact; you are truly unique and special amongst the billions. You are not one in a million. You are one in 108 billion! Congratulations!

You are different to everyone else, but incredibly you are also made up of exactly the same small number of ingredients. Almost 99% of the mass of your human body is made up of just six elements; oxygen, carbon, hydrogen, nitrogen, calcium and phosphorus. The remaining 1% is mostly composed of another five elements: potassium, sulphur, sodium, chlorine and magnesium. We are all made of the same stuff, just expressed differently. All 108 billion versions of human life have been made with just different mixes of the same elements, with each person being a slightly different recipe. Even those we call identical twins are not identical, as they have different DNA expressions.

It is common knowledge that everyone has fingerprint patterns that are unique, but did you know you can also be identified by your unique ear shape? No one else has ears just like you. Love your ears, they are special! The ridges, bumps and shape of the cartilage of your outer-ear is so unique that it may soon be one of the best ways to identify people, and at least as reliable as fingerprints. Scientists say it is already possible to recognise someone from even a low-quality picture of their ear with 99.6% accuracy. Start checking out people's ears, it's fascinating!

Your individuality does not, of course, stop at your fingerprints or the physical ear parts visible on your head. How you hear sounds and music is as unique as your fingerprints. Your skull's shape, size and bone density are all unique and create a resonant chamber which determines the sound signals that are sent to the brain according to how the waves vibrate or bounce around. The size of your skull, the amount of soft tissue around it and the hollow cavities inside mean the way it vibrates is different for every person. Like tiny tuning forks, the hairs in your ears quietly hum when stimulated and these vibrate in your head giving a sound that is completely your own. We tend to think of sound as something we hear and something making noise, but sound is just a vibration, or pressure waves, and the vibration is received in each person's ear and skull in a completely unique way.

The uniqueness of eyes is probably more widely understood than the individuality of ears, and in the field of eye recognition there are many advances in technology that are able to analyse a person's eyes in order to prove their identity. The retina, the part at the very back of your eye where light rays focus, has a pattern of blood vessels unique to you. In fact, the retina is the only place in your body where doctors can see a snapshot of your central nervous system without opening you up.

Computers today can identify a person on a crowded city street just by the way they walk, as every human has a unique walking gait because of the subtle differences in our bone structure, muscles and our sense of balance. Hard to tell from the human eye sometimes, but computers can break down the way you move into a set of numbers that are unique to you. We all have our own style, way of moving, and a numerical walking password. Scientists in Finland have recently discovered we all have our own unique dancing style, too.

Think for a moment about the pattern of bumps and ridges on your tongue. They contain more than 10,000 taste buds filled with microscopic hairs which make it unique from any other of the 108 billion tongues that have ever been made, and even your voice is distinctive, formed by the unique length of your vocal tract. Your lips are also pretty special, like a unique barcode with their patterns of wrinkles as individual as your tongue. And our teeth have all evolved to be different, which is why dental records are often used in forensics to identify a dead body.

We smell different too, with our own unique individual odour print.

Even though diet changes can influence odours, everyone has a distinctive odour and it's even possible to identify individuals by looking at the fog of chemicals – the thermal plume – we leave in our wake as we move around. Scientists at the University of Bristol showed they could distinguish individuals by looking at a combination of 44 compounds secreted by the body which evaporate and surround us, and it's this unique scent trail that search dogs are able to detect.

And so it goes on. Our tears, our fingernails, our toes, our genitals, the pores on our nose, our heartbeats and even the proteins in our hair are all unique to us as individuals. Every part of us is in fact a one-off design. We certainly are a limited edition. A limited edition of one. An original piece of living art. Exact copying isn't something nature does, and nature has an astonishing capability to create.

> *"If you live in awareness, it is easy to see miracles everywhere. Each human being is a multiplicity of miracles. Eyes that see thousands of colours, shapes and forms; ears that hear a bee flying or a thunderclap; a brain that ponders a speck of dust as easily as the entire cosmos; a heart that beats in rhythm with the heartbeat of all beings. When we are tired and feel discouraged by life's daily struggles, we may not notice these miracles, but they are always there." – Thich Nhat Hanh*

Everything we can see of the human body is unique, and everything we cannot see; our brains, our hearts, our blood cells, our gut, everything inside us is also a bespoke unique-to-us design. Your genetic coding is the formula that tells your cells how to build, and pairs of your DNA's building blocks become code that is the blueprint for everything in your physical design that makes you unique. There are nearly 21,000 human genes on 23 chromosomes created from about 3 billion bases, and no other human being will have the exact same pattern of DNA as you. We are evolving from the same ingredients but are different expressions of humanness.

As our thoughts and emotions are created by our bodies, it makes sense that how we think and how we feel will also be different from every other human being. We are basically a composition of chemicals and electric charges, all 'being' or doing this human experience differently.

Whatever you believe about life and its origins, it would seem nonsensical to believe anything other than it was intended to be that way. You were designed to be different, to be unique, to be a one-off creation. You're supposed to be different to everyone else. You are truly one in 108 billion and no person who is alive today – or who has ever lived or whoever will live – is the same as you. Well done! You are spectacularly unique.

So, first things first, as you start working through the SYSO System, take a few moments to really appreciate the amazingness of your bespoke, one-off design. Really appreciate the remarkable one-in-all-the-lifetimes creation that you are.

EXERCISE 1
Appreciate Your Uniqueness

Find somewhere quiet and without distraction. Relax and appreciate the magnificent design you are.

Appreciate your uniqueness. Be still and breathe deeply and slowly, in through your nose and out through your mouth.

Each breath in is bringing you new oxygen to energise every cell in your body, and each breath out is getting rid of waste in the form of carbon dioxide.

Imagine all the negative thoughts and toxins leaving your body as waste with each exhale. Appreciate the beautiful gifts of your breathing and your heart beating.

Each day you will take about 23,000 breaths and your heart will beat about 100,000 times, without requiring you to consciously do anything. That's pretty impressive, don't you think?

Become more aware of the uniqueness of your ears, your eyes, your fingerprints, your tongue, your skin.

Think about the system that you are, where each unique piece plays an important part in the whole system.

Think about your blood, the river of your life, flowing around your vessels and how incredible this system is.

Be grateful for your 37 trillion active cells, all working together to make you unique.

You're an amazing creation. Breathe deeply and appreciate your unique self. You are astonishing. You were intended to be different and just the way you are. Your uniqueness is your gift. Breathe and say thank you for what you have been given. Your difference is your advantage. Your difference is your power. Say a big thank you for your difference and for your potential. Carry on taking deep breaths in and long slow relaxing breaths out, feeling grateful and simply repeating the words 'Thank you' until you are ready to finish.

Thank you. Thank you. Thank you. Thank You. Thank You.

All life is unique

In all our unique forms, as humans, we are not alone in living on this planet. We share Earth with an estimated 8.7 million other species of life all of which are also individually different by design. Three-quarters of these other life forms, the majority of which are insects, are believed to be on land and only one-quarter are in the oceans. Some 86% of all plants and animals on land and 91% of those in the seas have yet to be named and catalogued. What we do definitely know for sure, however, is that every form is unique. That is a lot of difference. Difference *is* life.

We should question any thoughts about humans somehow being superior to other forms of life. What if everything was different, but completely equal and just as valuable as any other part of the whole system of life? It seems incredibly arrogant to assign 'superiority' to anything in nature. We are all part of the universe. As humans, we tend to think of ourselves as individual and separate and it may well be this delusion of separateness and sense of hierarchy which is at the heart of many of our emotional problems. We will explore this further throughout the book and especially in Step 6 when we look at the interconnectedness of all life.

Humans are relative newcomers. We have only lived for a fraction of the time this planet has existed, and the history of all animals that we have recorded from fossils is only about 15% of the recorded history of all life on Earth. The deeper history of life is microorganisms like bacteria, algae and protozoans and if the history of our planet to date was represented by 24 hours, human presence on this planet would only be for about the last 1 minute and 18 seconds. There is a lot more to life than just humans. There is a lot more to life than just us.

If we look beyond our little Planet Earth, even though there is much still being discovered, we know that all planets and all solar systems are different in each galaxy, and there are billions of galaxies in our universe. Nothing is the same as anything else. Everything is different. Everything is unique.

The bottom line is that nature is differences. Life and nature is diversity. It was designed to be that way and we should celebrate this diversity. It truly is a remarkable design and manufacturing story. Human production quantities are enormous, with 350,000 new babies born every day, yet the products remain bespoke and unique.

"Strength lies in differences, not in similarities." – Stephen Covey

EXERCISE 2
Build Your Sensory Awareness

Take a for few moments to think about the uniqueness that is everything in nature.

Then focus specifically on each of your senses in turn.

1. Think about your **sight**. Look around, see what you can see, the colours, shades, textures, any movement. There is always

more to see. Keep looking. Try and look for something new in the same situation. The diversity and variety is amazing but what's more incredible is that we, as humans, can see so little of what is actually 'there', probably much less than 1% of the entire electromagnetic spectrum.

2. Think about your **hearing** and all the sounds you are aware of and how the sound is changing and moving. Be aware of the pitch, the tempo, the loudness, the timbre, the duration, the source of the soundwaves and how they are reaching you. Think about how these sounds make your feel. Practise listening more acutely. We are limited in what we can actually hear, in the same way we are limited in what we can see. Humans can only hear in a range of frequencies estimated at less than 1% of the entire acoustic spectrum. Think about what else you aren't hearing that other forms of life perhaps are.

3. Think about **tastes** and how you can determine different flavours, and how the saliva in your mouth is generated even in anticipation of some foods. Think about the textures of food and how easy it is to chew, and be aware of taste that lingers after you have swallowed your food.

4. Think about **smell**. Humans detect smells by inhaling air that contains odour molecules, which then bind to receptors inside the nose, relaying messages to the brain. Most scents are composed of many odorants and when you smell chocolate, for example, you are smelling hundreds of different odour molecules.

5. Think about your sense of **touch** and the feelings you have. Think about how you experience touch. Touch your face, your fingernails, the different texture in your knuckles, your palms and the back of your hand. Touch your hair, your eyelashes and your clothes. Feel the differences.

Now reflect on this exercise and be grateful for the ability you have to process life through your senses. If you are fortunate to have all your senses working well, appreciate many are less fortunate. Become more aware of, and grateful for, the capacity of your senses.

You are an incredible force of nature. Start noticing it more. Notice your place in the system of nature. Notice leaves, flowers, bees, birds, clouds, trees, grass, soil. The more you look at nature the more you will see and appreciate its astonishing design and diversity and the more you will appreciate being a part of life. Think about the tides, the clouds, the weather patterns, the visible sky, the wind, and think about your home, the planet which is rotating once every 24 hours at about 1600 km per hour.

"If you aren't inspired, look again." – Paul Smith, designer

Different but equal

Become more aware of being different but also know that everyone is equal. Rather than comparing yourself to others, focus instead on comparing yourself to your previous self, to the person you were. This is at the heart of what personal growth and development is all about. Focus on being the best version of your unique self and not on what other people are doing or how they are living; we all have our own unique set of qualities, thoughts, beliefs, emotions and values.

It's only when we start comparing components of one person to components of another that we start thinking of one person being 'better' than another. If we compare height, for example, we can decide who is taller or shorter, but height is only one tiny component of any human. A tall person might be tallest, but maybe much less able in other areas. They might have poorer hearing, sight, taste, feeling capability, a smaller brain structure, less blood cell vitality, weaker vascular design, neuron size, speed of sight and so on. We have so many components, functions and individual capabilities and everyone is different in every area.

It's healthy to compete but winning in one area doesn't mean winning overall. Nobody can be the 'most' in every area as we all have different capabilities and capacities. We're culturally programmed to compete, which is valuable and helps raise standards, but we need to appreciate we're only competing in specific aspects of ourselves. This is especially important for children to realise as they develop, that the best is only really important in terms of the 'best you' as there will always be some part or capability of you measured against someone else that will be 'better' or 'worse'.

Overall as a human, you are equal in life. Everyone has some capability, whether realised or not, in which they could be considered 'better' compared to others. Instead of comparing ourselves to measures – often physical and material – that we have been culturally programmed to compare against, what if we focused more on human qualities like kindness, compassion and gratitude? Our capacity in these areas which are non-physical is unlimited. If I'm short, I can only reach so high, but I have unlimited capacity and potential to be kind, compassionate and grateful.

Maybe there should be an Olympics for personal character or qualities? "The gold medal for kindness and compassion goes to..."

We are all different but we are all equal in the eyes of nature. The essence of being human is being different. Different but equal. This is life. When we are acutely tuned into our individuality and uniqueness, we are already more aware of life and it is in becoming more aware of ourselves, of others and of our environment that we can start to really grow as humans and to have the best life possible, maximising our capabilities and individual potential.

"Let's look for the things to be grateful for, and celebrate our differences – for wouldn't the world be rather boring if we were all the same?" – Richard Branson

Developing self-awareness

Awareness of our physical uniqueness is only the starting point. It's awareness of who we are as a person, our invisible forces, and how we behave which is at the core of all personal development and the power we have as human beings.

Without self-awareness, our thoughts, feelings and behaviour are controlled just by our unconscious beliefs, instincts, habits and values which we're unlikely to have ever questioned (see Step 2). If our quality of life is essentially about how we feel, then we need to have awareness about how and why we are feeling if we want to take charge and change (see Step 3).

If you want to be happier, you first need to be aware of how you are being, thinking, feeling and to take responsibility for this. It is actually more accurate and helpful to think about *doing* happiness rather than *being* happy, as feelings are things we do. We do depression, we do love, we do fulfilment. We are really humans 'doing' rather than humans 'being', and when we understand this we open the door to taking responsibility for – and realising we have the choice about – the feelings we 'do'.

EXERCISE 3
Become Aware of Emotional Triggers

Think of a time recently when you were angry or frustrated.

Now think of what happened just before that moment.

You didn't just get angry; some thought patterns kicked in and you 'did' a process in your brain. (More of what happens with these processes in Steps 2 and 3.)

Remember what triggered your anger thoughts. How did those thoughts make you feel?

How long did it last?

Draw a line across a blank sheet of paper representing the path of your anger from before the trigger to after the feeling had passed. Were you content and calm and then gradually you became angry or did you suddenly spike up and change your feelings immediately? Mark this path on your paper and write down the length of time these feelings lasted.

Then think about what happened to change your feelings over the course of your graph. Was there a distraction? Did you change your thoughts or perspective? Did you feel like your anger 'burnt out' or dissipated naturally? Did something external change your thoughts and feelings?

Your answers and the 'anger timeline' you have just drawn, don't have to be super precise – this is just an exercise to help you start tuning in to how you are feeling and why.

Becoming more aware of ourselves, what we are feeling and why, allows us to take charge of processing and managing the feelings we want.

It all starts with awareness.

We can't control that which is outside ourselves but through self-awareness we can control our *responses* and therefore have a choice over how we feel. This is the key to 'doing' happy. Choose happiness, choose to take control of your response and feelings. Choose to have 'response ability'. For example, if you want a better relationship, most people usually start focusing on what's wrong or at fault with their partners, when we should start with ourselves and awareness of how we are. If we begin with self-awareness and taking responsibility, we can truly be the masters of our experience.

Identify your own bullshit

The first step of change is to become more aware of our own bullshit. If you want to give up a habit that isn't serving you well, such as smoking, drugs or gambling, the more awareness you have about what drives you, how you are thinking, and the emotions you're feeling, the more you'll be able to change your behaviour and create a higher quality of life. Your behaviour is really just patterns of thinking, habits and emotions. The more able you are to understand how you are enacting these patterns and habits, the more easily you can create new ones. Change can actually happen instantly when you become more aware and take the right actions to change patterns that aren't helping you lead the life you want. Incredibly, most people don't really think much about *how* they are thinking, but rather about *what* they think, and they don't usually ask themselves or seek to understand why they behave the way they do.

Self-awareness is the starting platform from which to learn how to change. If I don't know my car tyres are low on air, I won't know to get them fixed. If I don't know my roof is leaking, I won't know to get a roofing contractor. If I don't know my blood sugar level, I can't know if I'm diabetic and if I don't know my beliefs are limiting me, I'm unlikely to realise my potential. The sooner we can become more aware, the better, or it will only be when we face a big problem in life that we'll be forced to.

Being aware of the invisible forces that shape our experience of life, such as our thoughts, beliefs, feelings, emotions, needs and energy, is the key foundation in being able to make significant changes. If you want to change how you think and feel, start by being more aware of your thoughts and the feelings you are experiencing. If you want to be more successful financially, physically, in relationships and in your work, then you need to be aware of exactly where you now are and where you would like to get to.

Often, we react to our emotions and feelings, but if we are aware of them and not at the mercy of them, we can take charge. If you want to change your world, the world going on outside, it starts by changing the world going on inside you. You see things, and people, not as they are, but rather as you are. It all starts with your inner world. Build awareness of yourself and take charge of growing and becoming more, and your outer world will change.

You have response ability

Think of a time when you felt really pissed off because of something someone said to you. What did they say? Were you really offended? Only you know exactly how you reacted then, or in other situations like this, but as you develop your awareness, you will start reacting differently and feeling differently. Firstly, you'll appreciate that other people's words and actions are not yours, unless you choose to take them on board. You can't control how others behave and what they say, but you can 100% control your reaction, and it's your choice of reaction that will determine your feelings. For example, words don't 'do' anything to you, only you can 'do' it to you, whatever you have decided 'it' is. You can't be offended by someone, you can only choose to take offence. By building awareness, you realise others' actions and words reflect what is going on in their heads and hearts and not yours. Can someone hurt you by something they say? Only if you allow it to. Ask yourself if you are going to allow something outside yourself to control how you feel?

Imagine someone approaches you who you think is very drunk and aggressive. You've seen them shout angrily and aggressively at others and now they approach you, asking loudly if you're colour blind because who else would wear shoes like yours? Are you going to allow what they say to affect what you feel about your shoe choice? What if you later found out they had a serious neurological illness, that they were dying slowly and had to take drugs which made them hallucinate and become wildly irrational and verbally aggressive? What would you think differently about the interaction? Likely you would feel sorry for them and not be at all bothered by whatever they'd said. The reality is we don't ever really know what's going on in other people's heads, and so it's crazy to give up your power to something outside yourself which you don't likely understand anyway.

It should already seem a little strange, the whole concept of allowing others to affect how you feel. Of course, we all feel frustrated and angry at times and people will do things that feel painful to you, especially in relationships and business, but the key is to understand or be aware of what is happening and why, and then take charge of the meaning you attach to this and choose your response. You'll learn much more about this and exercises to practise throughout the book, especially in Steps 2 and 3. If you follow the SYSO System, you'll be the boss of your own life experience, not at the mercy of things that happen 'to' you.

Clarity precedes success

If you're not achieving your goals in life, the first question to ask is are you really clear on what they are and why? You can never be too clear about your goals, and without absolute clarity on what you want to achieve, you're not going to get there. If you do know what you want but can't get seem to make progress, do you understand what's stopping you? It all starts with awareness and unblocking the bullshit blocks we have accumulated. Imagine I'm not happy in my relationship or my work or with my fitness (or all of these). Without knowing why, and without knowing clearly what I really want, I'll find myself very stuck and deeply unhappy.

"Our greatness lies not so much in being able to remake the world as being able to remake ourselves." – Mahatma Gandhi

You have everything you need within you, right here, right now, to make the changes you need in your life. Love yourself and your differences. Love others and their differences. It's miraculous that you, or any of us, even exist. Scientist Dr Ali Binazir says the chances of a particular sperm fertilising a particular egg for you to be born is 1 in 400 trillion. You are indeed a miracle and a very limited and special edition. You are exceptional.

EXERCISE 4
Notice Others' Uniqueness

Find somewhere comfortable to sit in a public place where there are plenty of people passing. A town centre, train station or park, for example.

Start noticing the uniqueness of every person. The uniqueness of faces, of height. All different, and all designed that way.

Now imagine you have the superpower of being able to see inside all these people, and think about how everything inside is also physically different.

After you have spent some time being aware of the physical uniqueness inside and out,

now think about and imagine the invisible and non-physical aspects of the people you are looking at. Imagine the thoughts, the feelings, the beliefs, the values of each person. Of course, you can only guess, but just let your imagination and awareness run loose and realise that the vast majority of what makes a person is actually invisible!

Celebrate uniqueness and celebrate the differences, and rather than judging and criticising others or yourself for not being the same, be grateful. Diversity is your power in life and we should embrace the differences rather than fight against nature's design.

> *"To be beautiful means to be yourself. You don't need to be accepted by others. You need to accept yourself. When you are born a lotus flower, be a beautiful lotus flower, don't try to be a magnolia flower. If you crave acceptance and recognition and try and change yourself to fit what other people want you to be, you will suffer all your life. True happiness and true power lie in understanding yourself, accepting yourself, having confidence in yourself." – Thich Nhat Hanh*

Self-awareness is your superpower

By now it should be loud and clear and I don't apologise for any repetition. The first foundation and step of the SYSO System is to become more *aware.* Become more aware of yourself, of your power, of others and of your environment. When you become more aware and notice more, you appreciate how incredible life really is. And when you do that, you'll feel grateful. And being grateful is a key to a very happy life. To not be aware, is to take things for granted which is the opposite of feeling grateful.

So, that all sounds good in theory, but how do you actually become more aware? You simply decide to! You choose to, and then you take action, and this book has the tools to help you take this action. The more aware you become the more you will discover how much there is to be aware of! Your life will be richer and you will be able to make changes you otherwise would probably never have realised were holding you back.

Human intelligence, unlike other forms of life, as far as we know, gives us a unique ability to observe ourselves and maintain perspective; we can look at our lives, and look ahead to evaluate options. It's a potential that is mostly unused by many people, and the first step is to realise that *we can be more aware.*

Decide now and start practising. Self-awareness allows you to appreciate your individualness (and everyone else's). It's an orientation, a quest to always keep building your awareness 'muscles', to be conscious of the physical, but also of the invisible forces in you. Self-awareness allows you to make changes in the thoughts, beliefs, and interpretations in your mind which affects your emotions and experience of life.

EXERCISE 5
Observe Your Thoughts

Sit comfortably with your feet flat on the floor and just breathe deeply and relax.

Read this and then follow the instructions with your eyes closed.

As you relax, imagine all the stresses draining away from your body and appreciate each breath bringing in new, fresh energy.

Focus on your breathing. Focus on feeling your chest moving with each breath and focus on the feeling of each exhale and release.

When you feel completely relaxed, think about what thoughts you're having. They're just thoughts, they are not you. Just observe them as if they are passing in front of you and then dissolving as they float on by.

Keep coming back to your breath if you get distracted or if you feel your mind racing or jumping around.

Simply quieten your mind, focus on your breathing and the thoughts you are watching as they come and go.

You can do this at any time and in any place and as you practise, you will be building your awareness muscle.

Until you are aware in the moment of your thoughts, emotions, language and behaviours, you will have difficulty making significant changes in your life.

As you build your self-awareness, you'll realise you are in control, and you'll choose how you want to think and feel and you'll empower yourself. You'll create your experience of life. Everyone has bad stuff happen in their life, but with greater self-awareness you can learn to see you that you're not a victim. In its truest sense, there are no victims, only volunteers. You have the power to choose how you are responding to anything outside yourself even if you can't control what has happened. When you are more self-aware, you are more understanding of others. You don't have to take on their crap or shrink yourself so they can feel better, but you can be more compassionate, and your relationships will improve dramatically as a result. We can't control a lot of what happens to us in life but we can *always control our response.*

As you go through the 7 steps of the SYSO System, you will see how becoming more self-aware is the critical first foundation from which you can start to build a new, higher quality of life. By being aware of how you are behaving, you can transform your experience of life. Wake up, tune in, become more aware of how you are being, how you are doing and you will start to expand your sense of what it is to be alive. Without knowing where you are, you can't work out where you want to be. Without realising what is holding you back, you can't move forward in the ways you want. Increased awareness will free you and give you the power to change the quality of your experience of being alive. If you can't see, and aren't aware of how you are, you can't change.

What's your personality type?

One useful tool in any self-awareness work to is to have a simple way you can think about different personality or behaviour types. As we know, we are all unique, and therefore technically there are more than 7 billion personality types, but it can be helpful to have a simple framework you can use to quickly assess personalities generally, even if the concept of personality types is a little contradictory.

There are many personality or psychometric tests available which have been developed over the years, and if you work for a large corporation you've likely been 'assessed' at some point. I like the simple, clear and easy to use frameworks, and in my experience for accurateness and simplicity a test called

DISC is good. Other well-known tests and models include Myers Briggs Type Indicator, Primary Colours Personality Test, Strength Finder, Wealth Dynamics, and the Enneagram model, although there are many more in a $2 billion market for 'assessing people'. Whichever test you use, remember it's just a guide as everyone has their own unique individual personality type, although they can be useful as a base for further exploration and becoming more aware of ourselves and understanding others.

The DISC tool is a behaviour assessment based on the theory of psychologist, William Marston, and which centres on four different personality types. These can broadly be classified as Dominance, Influence, Steadiness and Conscientiousness. The exercise involves a series of questions and four answer options which you place in priority according to how you believe the answers best describes you. The collective answers you give come together to rate you against four different measures. However, you can get a glimpse into these personality classifications by asking two simple questions, which will help you gain a good idea of your own, or someone else's, behaviour profile at a very basic, but useful, level. It's also good to remember that we may express a different type of personality in different environments, such as work or socially, so context is important.

EXERCISE 6
What's Your Personality Type?

Start with a blank sheet of paper and a pen and ask yourself the following two questions:

Q1 – Do you consider yourself more outgoing or introverted?
Draw a vertical line in the centre of your page. At the top end of the line write 'outgoing'. At the bottom end of the line write 'introverted' and then, using your best intuitive estimate, think where you would place yourself on this line/axis in terms of whether you consider yourself more extrovert or introvert.

<u>Q2 – When doing tasks, are you more focused on the people and their feelings or on getting the task done?</u>
Now draw a horizontal line across the middle of vertical line you have made, and on this line, write 'task' on the left end and 'people' on the right.

On this horizontal line/axis, think about whether you prioritise people and their feelings or getting the task done, and where you would position yourself on that axis. There's no need to try and be 'exact' and there is no correct answer.

You will now have two lines crossing each other in the centre and four quadrants, and the answers you have given to these two questions above will determine which quadrant your personality likely fits.

Everyone is different and within any quadrant there will be nuances.

It is situational of course too, but as a basic introduction this is a useful initial insight and self-awareness tool.

If you positioned yourself in the top left quadrant you would likely be someone who's behaviour is outgoing and focused primarily on getting the task done, and if you see yourself as in the top right quadrant, you're likely outgoing but focus primarily on people. In the bottom right, the priority is people and you consider yourself more reserved or introverted, and in the bottom left, you're introverted but focused on the task and getting results.

The four quadrants are not exact, and the tool is more about priorities and variations in degree, so this is definitely not about labelling or rigidly classifying behaviour. Rather it is just one tool that can be helpful in creating awareness. The benefit is to invite thinking about how you and others will behave in certain situations.

If you would like something simpler, which I use informally and especially in business, I have created my own simple four quadrant fast assessment called the Action and Results Assessment (ARA). It also starts with two simple lines/axis as with the DISC profiling:

EXERCISE 7
The Action and Results Assessment (ARA)

Draw a vertical line on a page of blank paper. At the top of the line write 'Results Focused' and at the bottom, 'Process Focused'. Where would you put yourself on that simple scale? This exercise is about you, but you can also think about others you interact with and especially in a business environment.

Now draw another line, this time a horizontal one across the page passing through the middle of the vertical line and about the same length.

At the end of this line on the right side, write 'Takes Action' and at the end of the line on the left write 'Likes Discussion'.

Again, think first of yourself and where you would position yourself on that scale and then you can think of others you interact with.

As in the DISC example, you'll now have two lines which cross and make four quadrants and you can assess yourself, and others, as to whether they focus more on the results or the process and if their style is more action-orientated or if they like talking about things.

Remember, this is a just a very basic generalisation and people can show different styles in different situations depending on what's at stake and any other pressures they feel.

This ARA is most suited for basic assessments in a business/work environment and if you start using this informally, you'll start to think differently about how you work with others.

I like to work with 'results focused' and 'takes action' type personalities but different situations are better suited to different personality types. In any team, it's usually useful to have a blend of complimentary personality styles and there's no better or worse type; this is simply an exercise in becoming more aware of how we and others are behaving.

Another very simple assessment, devised by Richard Bandler (cofounder of Neuro Linguistic Programming), is useful when meeting with any potential business partner. Richard is a straight-talking, no bullshit kind of guy (who I thoroughly recommend going to see live if you get the chance) and is a legend in the study of the mind and language patterns.

Bandler advises that all you need to do is take any potential business partner to a Chinese restaurant that has a huge menu and then just watch how that person makes their food choice! He looks for fast, self-assured, decision-making rather than dithering "what are you having?" indecisiveness. This, of course, is not a recognised formal psychometric test but it is brilliant in its simplicity; as successful people generally make quick decisions, while unsuccessful people generally make slow decisions (and often change them quickly). This makes great sense as an easy assessment tool. Try it next time you're eating out. It's a great way to practice tuning into higher levels of awareness of human behaviour, although it should be stressed that this might not be a particularly useful assessment technique for a potential romantic partner. I would not be married if it was!

Aiming to understand others, rather than judging their behaviour, will change your relationships dramatically, although the starting point is always understanding ourselves first, and there are many ways to practise this.

Write to bring clarity

To bring focus and clarity, writing stuff down is an incredibly powerful practice and it's smart to make a habit of doing this. It doesn't require you to be endlessly writing and it can be in whichever format is easiest; pen and paper or on your phone or an electronic device. The act of writing and taking notes makes the invisible thoughts visible and helps direct your mind (see more in Step 2).

EXERCISE 8
Use Writing To Focus

The purpose of this exercise is to help focus your thoughts, and to become more aware of how you are 'doing' your life. Here are some examples of the things you can write. Of course, you can write whatever is important to how you think, feel and the goals you have.

Decide how you're going to write; will it be electronically on your phone? Or in a notebook? Start making notes, not long sentences. It is just to bring focus.

Here are some examples of areas you can start with:

1. Journal your feelings. Perhaps note the time, the place, what you are feeling and why you believe you are feeling this way. Find a simple way of noting this that works for you.

2. Create a list of qualities you value most in human behaviour.

3. Write a list of what is important to you, and the life you want.

4. Start writing specific goals for your future.

5. Take a daily audit of how much you laughed and smiled.

6. Make a list of things you are grateful for.

7. Write a list of the most important people in your life and why.

8. Write a letter to yourself as if you were at the very end of your life. What have you learnt about yourself and life and what would you do differently, knowing what you know now?

These are just some examples of areas in which you can start making notes, but the key is to start! Once you begin, you will feel more focused and by writing these thoughts down, you are taking charge in the process of building your self-awareness.

How do you talk to yourself?

Do you pay much attention to how you talk to yourself? Self-talk as we shall cover in Step 2 is a critical component of how you think about who you are and how you're directing yourself in life. You might never actually have thought about it much, but we tend to talk a lot to ourselves in our heads. Being aware of what and how we are talking and whether this is helpful or not, can help us then build a more empowering, positive and fun dialogue with ourselves.

Tune into the language you and others use. Language makes a huge difference to how we feel. Use more emphatic, positive, enthusiastic, empowering language and your life will change through that alone. Not only will upbeat language feel better but your biochemistry changes when you use more uplifting words. So, start now, and become acutely aware of the language you use. Try and think of more words to describe any strong positive emotions you experience. Build your vocabulary and expand your life.

"Your results are an expression of your level of awareness." – Bob Proctor

If you have read this chapter, Step 1 of the SYSO System, and practised the exercises, you'll already be building your awareness muscles and life will be different. Regularly remind yourself that you are unique and special, that everyone is unique and special and we are all equal and essential parts of life. You are unique, you are loved, you are enough, and *all* you need is within you.

As a human you are doing living, you are doing behaviour. When you understand that and are aware of what you're doing and why, you can take responsibility for your life and start effecting changes more easily. You are not so much a human being but rather a human doing, and when you understand you are 'doing' your behaviour, you can choose to 'do' more empowering and effective behaviour.

Many people are living in a world of self-victimisation, where they are feeding a story of what happened in their past and how bad or unfair it was. They stay the victim rather than taking responsibility for how they can choose to feel by changing the meaning they give to things. When you're aware of your thoughts, words, emotions and behaviour, you'll be able to change the direction of your future. Society, especially with social media, encourages us to become increasingly self-absorbed and less self-aware but you're reading this book so you already appreciate how important it is to become more aware and you'll already be reaping the rewards of improving yourself.

"Every time you are tempted to react in the same old way, ask if you want to be a prisoner of the past or a pioneer of the future." – Deepak Chopra

As you build your awareness muscles, you will also become more aware of others and the world around you. Realising that there is so much we don't know makes us less rigidly opinionated and opens our hearts and minds, allowing us to feel grateful and curious and keep perspective. We become more understanding of others and less judgemental; showing compassion is our core human nature. We are here sharing this rotating planet with so much more than just other people and this planet is sharing the universe with more than just other planets. By becoming more aware, you'll be able to appreciate the perfect unique beauty that is life. Smile, appreciate all the beauty and relax into knowing we can't know everything in this lifetime. Enjoy the journey and your new expanded filter for your experience of being alive.

"Everything in the universe is within you." – Rumi

STEP 2
Manage Your Mind

"Training and managing your own mind is the most important skill you could ever own, in terms of both happiness and success." – T. Harv Eker

When you actively decide to manage your mind and be in control of how you think, rather than just reacting to the thoughts you have, you'll transform how you feel and what you do. It really is that straightforward. How you think affects what you feel, and how you feel affects what you do, and what you feel and do is your life! So, if you change how you think, you will change your life.

We're mostly taught 'what' to think and sometimes 'why' to think it, but there isn't much focus on the 'how' of thinking. How to think more effectively and deliberately to make the most of your life. 'How to Manage Your Mind' should be a compulsory part of all school curricula, and a focus for parents and caregivers at home.

You don't need to go to India to find yourself (although why not still go and be inspired anyway?), you don't need to have millions in the bank to be happy (but why not have that and more anyway?), and you don't need to have a phenomenal passionate and loving relationship to feel really alive and be happy (although I thoroughly recommend that too). You just need to change how you think, and you will realise you aren't stuck, broken or lost, you were right here all along, just needing to be uncovered and to become the manager of your mind rather than a casual labourer to it. When you work on how you think, you'll grow and 'become more' as a person, which, as opposed to 'getting more', is the key to feeling fulfilled in life.

Train your brain

There's often an assumption that thinking is just something you do automatically because of the brain you were born with, and that you can't, or don't need to, train your brain to think in a better way. Most people are just living by reacting to, rather than being the manager of, their thoughts. These thoughts are in control, not the other way around, but we can train ourselves to think more effectively for the life we want, and it all starts with awareness. Become more aware of what thinking is, and take control of the patterns which are created in your brain, and you'll be in the driving seat of your life and your journey.

> *"Awareness is perhaps the most important mental function that can change the brain. If a magic genie appeared and granted you only one wish for your brain fitness, go with awareness." – John Assaraf*

We often ask or are asked, "What do you think?" about something and then we just exchange opinions with each other and debate or argue over the 'why', trying to position our own opinion as the winner. In the Western world especially, we're generally very good at reasoning, critical thinking and memory recall, but usually much less aware of the how or process of thinking. Commit to learning and developing how you think and discover your ability to condition your brain and its thinking patterns for success so you can choose to feel happy anytime you like. You'll also become more understanding of how others are thinking, and so become more understanding of their behaviour, which leads to more tolerance, and a greater ability to have influence and enjoy better relationships in all areas of your life.

Thinking is the programming or software creator of your brain, which determines what you feel and do. The software runs us, but other than the basic inbuilt human survival and operating programmes which we all have, most of the rest of our software has been developed without our being aware it is even software. We just think it's the way we're made, but our behaviour is not who we are at our core. Our behaviour is just the result of the programming we have taken on and the thinking patterns of this programming. If you find yourself judging other people, it's usually their behaviour and their programming you're judging, and not the person. You're also judging it through the filter of your own programming; I love my children but I sometimes don't love their behaviour!

Mind health

We understand about training our bodies for health, but we seldom talk about training, or programming, our minds for health, yet mind health will determine the quality of our life. For most people, mental health still has negative connotations; implying there's a physical problem in someone's head, or that something is broken. People are described as 'having' a mental illness or 'having' mental problems. Of course, people can 'have' physical problems in all parts of their bodies and some people do have a physical or technical hardware problem in their heads through injury or structural defect, but the vast majority of us haven't got a mental 'illness'. We just haven't learnt how to 'do' the process of thinking more effectively in a way which makes us feel great and empowered to make the most of our lives.

"I am not what happened to me. I am what I choose to become." – *Carl Jung*

Our brain is a processor, and it's running processes. We need to work on the processes and how we are doing them, because when we change these, we change our feelings and we change our life. If we are doing a process, we can do it differently when we know how to. We might have a virus, some 'wiring' ineffectiveness or a chemical imbalance in our brains and bodies, but we can recondition our thinking to create new processes, or patterns, which will change the 'wiring' and the chemical mix, which will change our feelings. We can upgrade our software to upgrade our life.

Most people aren't aware of their thinking processes, or believe it's just 'not that easy' to make changes to their thinking. People who are struggling to change some behaviour, such as smoking or overeating, often say things like "I just can't help it," or "I have an addiction." If we take smoking as an example, stopping should be very straightforward. The responsibility for lifting a cigarette and putting it in your mouth is controlled only by you and I have never heard anyone proclaim someone else is forcing cigarettes into their mouth, lighting them and making them inhale. The excuse is usually that they've tried but just can't stop, or that they're 'addicted'.

When we assign blame to something outside of our control for something we want to change, or don't like about ourselves, we can then say "It's not my fault" or "I'm an addict" and this can take away our responsibility and our ability, or the power we have, to make the changes. *Taking 100% responsibility for what we do and how we feel is the foundation of creating the life we want.* We can't control things outside ourselves but we can control our inner world and we can take responsibility for how we think and how we feel. We have the power over our thinking, so all that we have to do is use this power, and not give it up.

The brain is designed to work for us, and it's our unconscious (we'll learn more about this later), which runs most of our behaviour like an autopilot. We just need to give directions and tell the brain to do the processes that will cause the thoughts, feelings and behaviour we want. These forces for thinking, feeling and behaving are all inside us. Everything we need is within us right here, right now.

"I don't fix problems. I fix my thinking. Then problems fix themselves." – Louise L. Hay

Taking charge

When we take charge of our thinking, we can train our minds to take action that will get the results we want in any area of our life. What we don't change, we are actively choosing. And we need to train our brains to focus on the solutions, and not waste time overanalysing the problems. The most common areas people usually want to change are their health, relationships and finances. Most people know how to change, but maybe haven't a strong enough reason why they want the change or they have an emotional block or resistance which is getting in their way. We shall learn in this Step how to deal with these invisible blocks to taking action and we'll practice some exercises to train our minds for successful change, in whatever area of our life we choose.

Often, when we talk about anything to do with our brains or minds, the implication is that this is a highly specialised area where only psychologists or neuroscientists or professors in white lab coats can help 'fix' our 'mental problems', or that a long course with a psychotherapist or counsellor is necessary. The study of the brain is for sure a complex area and there are some exceptionally clever people working in this field who we should be very grateful for. However, to train your brain to work in a better, more practical way, or to manage your mind for happiness, isn't that complicated. You just need to know what to do, and then do it. You can sort yourself out and it doesn't have to take long.

You don't need to understand how everything works to get your brain thinking effectively. I don't need to understand the intricate details of how a plane works to fly me from London to New York or how the inner processor in my smartphone is working when I call my wife from the other side of the world. I just need to know what I want to do, where I want to go to, how to get the flight, or what number to dial for the phone call. If I want to get fit, I don't need to understand how every ligament, tendon and muscle works, I just need to know what to do and how to get myself fit. I do need some understanding but I really just need a plan of action to get results and effective thinking to make it happen. I need *action-activating thoughts*, and I can easily train myself for those.

You don't need to be a neuroscientist to change your brain 'wiring', you just need to be your own 'neuro manager', the manager of your mind. You don't need a PhD in psychology to have sufficient understanding of the brain's basic workings to maximise its effectiveness. Even psychologists and neuroscientists haven't got a complete understanding of how this most powerful computer – our brain – works anyway. There is some incredible research and study going on, making new discoveries, but there's still a lot about the workings of our brains we don't understand. Like life itself; the quest for understanding the mind may be a never-ending pursuit and there's great freedom in realising we just don't know everything. Some things in life may not be understandable in this lifetime. Study and inquire as much as you choose to, of course, but in the meantime the SYSO System is about focusing on the life you want *now*. The SYSO System is about *very* practical psychology.

So, start right now. Commit to training and managing your mind for success. The problem isn't that you aren't 'smart' enough, or that you're faulty, or because something awful happened in your life. You just haven't programmed your brain to do what it's capable of. The reality is that you're using only a tiny amount of your capability and likely not giving yourself clear enough direction. Let's change that.

"The primary cause of unhappiness is never the situation but your thoughts about it." – Eckhart Tolle

Your brain didn't come with an instruction manual

Don't beat yourself up if your current programming isn't working for you; we need to know how to use the amazing brain we have, but it didn't come with an instruction manual and we're not usually taught formally at school about brain management and how to think. We may have taken on programming that was perhaps helpful for a different time or from people around us, rather than actively taking charge and programming ourselves for the life we want.

Opinions and other people's beliefs are pushed to us in the media, by family and our peer groups but do we stop and ask where these opinions have come from and why they are believed? You can either be unaware and programmed by the messages around you or you can take charge and programme yourself for the life you want. Which would you prefer?

Our different brains

Our education system has traditionally put a lot of emphasis on generalised and conventional tests to measure people's 'Intelligence Quotient', but these tests only measure one dimension of something that has been defined as intelligence. There are many types of intelligence in human life and in nature, and everyone is equally intelligent when we broaden the definition to allow for different capabilities and capacities. We know every brain – and the processes within each – is unique, yet society is increasingly using labels to classify people if they're different from some decided upon 'norm'.

Labels like Autism, ADHD, Dyslexia, Bipolar, Impulse Control Disorder, OCD, and Asperger's Syndrome, for example, are ascribed increasingly frequently, and the number of these labels seems to be growing all the time. Labelling someone tends to focus on what they can't do in one area rather than revealing what they can do in other areas. It doesn't seem to be very helpful to single out someone, especially a child, and tell them they 'have' some sort of 'learning disability' when they actually have unique processing skills probably superior to the average in some other area of their capacity.

For example, ADHD is frequently used to label someone who just might be super bright and needs lots of stimulation. In school, could it be that the teacher has a 'Lack of Stimulating Teaching Disorder' rather than the child 'having' ADHD? To describe someone as having a deficit of attention, we must be comparing them to someone else, or likely in this case, comparing to an 'average', yet there are many super-bright children, eager for new stimulation but who are held back because the standard of average might be fairly low in their taught group. It all depends on what is being measured.

We all have a unique comfort level for stimulation as all our brains are different. For example, we all have a different rate of words per minute that feels right to speak at, and a number of words per minute we can comfortably process in terms of listening. Most humans speak at around 100–250 words a minute, and when thinking, form words somewhere between 1000 and 3000 words per minute. Imagine if someone speaking at 100 words a minute is communicating to someone with a 3000 words a minute thinking and processing speed? We've all experienced what it's like listening to someone who speaks very slowly compared to how we process their words, especially when the topic is not that interesting to us. It can be torture! Similarly, processing fast talking can be difficult if your processor is designed for slower input speeds, but it doesn't mean the person with the fast (or slow) brain has a syndrome! They just have a fast (or slow) words processor.

Exceptional ways of thinking

We know that we're all different and in different ways (Step 1), and we should do more to harness peoples specialness, rather than label individuals in a negative way. It would be more helpful to describe people as having their own unique learning differences and to acknowledge that everybody can benefit from support and personalised learning plans rather than telling a child they have 'special needs' or assigning stigmatic labels. We're all special and we all have special needs unique to us. The entire class at school has special, or individual, needs. We should encourage our children to find their individual strengths within their amazing uniqueness and help them understand that they do not 'have' these disability labels, they are 'doing' different ways of thinking and 'doing' certain behaviours, not 'having' them. They are running processes that can be changed.

Moreover, in terms of many of these people we have classified as having 'learning disabilities', we could probably learn a lot from how they think, as they often have particularly advanced skills in certain areas. They don't have a learning disability they have an exceptional learning ability, just in a different way from the average way we expect people to think.

Take the example of Stephen Wiltshire, diagnosed with autism at age three, but became famous for producing highly detailed artwork scenes after just a brief glance at the original. His teachers didn't know what to do with him at school. Stephen didn't have a disability, he had an exceptional learning ability (ELA) and perhaps his teachers had a disability in being unable to recognise it! Labelling children, singling them out and telling them they have a disability is not helpful. They will often start describing themselves as having the label and using language like "I am" autistic, "I am" dyslexic, which becomes part of their self-identity, when really what is happening is that they are 'doing' autism or 'doing' dyslexia etc. They are all amazing unique human beings, just thinking in particular ways and many just need to understand how they can channel their abilities effectively, like Stephen Wiltshire.

We are all weaker and stronger in some areas of our learning than others, because we are all different, but everyone has an ELA and probably more than one. There are many very talented famous people who have been labelled in their lives as having learning disabilities or special needs. Rather than 'learning disability', I think it would be more accurate to describe these people as being gifted with an 'exceptional way of thinking'. They all have ELAs. Look at Richard Branson (dyslexia), Steven Spielberg (dyslexia), Jamie Oliver (dyslexia), Emma Watson (ADHD), Maria Carey (bipolar), Bill Gates (ADHD), Charles Schwab (dyslexia), Erin Brockovich (dyslexia), Justin Timberlake (OCD), Michael Phelps (ADHD) Orlando Bloom (dyslexia), Jim Carrey (ADHD), Jennifer Aniston (dyslexia), Leonardo DiCaprio (OCD) and Keira Knightley (dyslexia). There are many more public figures we could add to the list and all around us people have been labelled as 'having' some special learning needs, when we all have special learning needs as we're all unique.

Neuroplasticity

Scientists used to believe that your brain can't change much, and that you were born with a biologically predetermined brain. More recent research, however, shows that the brain can and does change throughout life, not just with the ways of thinking but physically too; this process is called neuroplasticity, as we change in response to our behaviour, environment and thinking. We can grow more brain cells, and create more and better connections between cells.

The brain can and does change. It is a tool to work for us. It just needs our management and direction. Its primary objective is to help us process information in order to stay alive and be energy efficient in doing so. It has a negativity bias built in to help with survival that evolved through what was a dangerous world for our ancestors and so it is constantly looking out for threats and what is wrong. It isn't naturally programmed to look for what is right; what's right isn't a danger, so it's acutely sensitive to bad experiences as it wants to protect us and this may explain why we tend to hang onto bad experiences for so long.

Most of us, when we have good experiences are not good at installing these and learning from the good. We need to wire ourselves proactively to feel good quicker. We need to notice what's right more often, rather than being hunters of faults. Our brain needs to be trained to see the positive. Fortunately, nature has given us the ability to wire our brains and install programming for whatever feelings we want.

"Your mind is programmable. If you're not programming your mind, someone else will program it for you" – Jeremy Hammond

Programming

Think of two new-born babies. All they essentially want to do is feed, sleep, pass their waste, keep warm, move, and be held, and if they don't get these things they get agitated and cry. This is the basic inbuilt programming of being human, or the functioning and survival programme we all have from birth. As they grow, each child will develop a different set of things they believe and value in their world. They'll become wired differently based on their experiences, their environment, their parents and their peer group. For most people as they develop, the programming happens without them being aware it's even programming, but it happens anyway, whether they're in charge or not as the brain needs 'software' to know what to do.

To become a great manager of our mind, first we need to become more aware that we are in control of our programming. We then need to guard our minds from unhelpful opinions and beliefs that attempt to programme us without permission. Think of your brain like it's your beautiful, unique house that you built, full of amazing detail and decor. Say you had a party and different people wanted to come in and make trouble, or change the atmosphere or start being destructive. Would you let anyone into your house, at any time, to do whatever they wanted to do? Of course you wouldn't. You would stand guard and decide who came into your home, and in the same way we should stand guard at the door of our mind. We all have lots of thoughts, and the key is to channel the effective ones and let the others go on by. You're the bouncer of your mind, the curator of the party, the manager of your guest list. So, decide now, as you read this, that you are going to take control of your mind and your brain programming. You are going to manage and direct your brain because now you know you can. You are not going to negotiate with it, you are going to direct it.

EXERCISE 9
Decide to Be in Charge of Your Mind

Find a place where you won't be disturbed.

Decide now that you are going to be in charge. You know your brain is designed to work for you. You are going to give your brain directions. It is designed as a tool to work for you.

Write down the following phrase which you are going to make the primary programming incantation for your mind. (More on incantations to follow.)

You are going to repeatedly speak this phrase with intensity and physically embed it as your new programming. You will use the clear powerful words, your body and your emotion to install this programme so your mind works for you:

"MY brain works FOR me,
I control MY brain and direct it to SERVE me,
I manage MY brain to get the results I want
I do not negotiate with my brain."

Repeat this multiple times, stick it on a post-it note above your desk, in your car, make it a screensaver, wherever you need to put it as a reminder that you are in charge and you are going to train your brain for the life you want.

Managing your mind starts with giving clear direction. If you haven't given clear direction you can't complain about the output. You are in charge, you give the directions. You don't negotiate with your brain, it is a tool that works for you.

Become an observer of your thoughts

If you have a brain there will be thoughts. Neuroscientists don't really know where thoughts actually come from, but people have about 60,000–80,000 thoughts a day and most of them are the same thoughts as yesterday! We have thoughts about all kinds of seemingly random stuff and we should be grateful we have the capacity to have such a never-ending flow, but the key to effective mind management is to filter and channel these thoughts and create an environment for empowering and useful new thoughts to develop.

First, become an observer of your thoughts (see Exercise 5 in Step 1) rather than reacting to them or feeling overwhelmed by the quantity and seeming randomness. When we're aware, we can decide to use the thoughts that are helpful for our clear goals, and just let the thoughts that aren't relevant or helpful pass by or dissolve. They will naturally pass anyway if we don't keep stoking them by giving them unnecessary attention. When we have focus, we know which thoughts are helpful and which aren't and this is a key foundation for all successful mind management. There is so much going on in our thoughts, unless we become great at filtering and focusing, our head will be full of chatter and overwhelm, with brain cells just firing away and creating all kinds of patterns, but not efficiently and not generating effective creative thoughts for our goals.

Celebrate your capacity to create thoughts, and to be able to just observe them. Don't feel bad or guilty if you have thoughts you wish you didn't have – everyone has these, they're just thoughts. Thoughts don't mean anything; they're not who you are, they come and go all the time. When you practise observing your thoughts from a distance, you're watching them and therefore they can't be you. Let the thoughts flow, some will be helpful and some will not. The aim is to have a directed mind, not a directionless, busy and confused mind.

Give your brain focus, or targets for your thoughts. Live with a directed mind. You are the director and you give the directions, so start by asking yourself what life you want and describe it as clearly as you can. People often describe what they don't want but the key is having *clarity on what you do want* otherwise your brain will be confused. If I went to the supermarket and my wife told me not to get milk, oranges and bread, is that going to help me buy what we need? The unconscious mind doesn't understand negatives and it won't be helpful to tell it what you don't want. Clarity is essential and you must tell your unconscious mind what you *do* want.

How your brain works

Your brain, as we already said, is a processor, constantly processing. It's the most complex part of our bodies, weighing on average in an adult around 1.5 kg, and is made mostly of water and fat. If it loses blood for 8–10 seconds you will lose consciousness. After 4–6 minutes without oxygen, it begins to die. It generates 10–20 watts of power when we are awake, which is enough power for a lightbulb, and at birth it's about a quarter of the size of an average adult brain, doubling in size in the first 12 months. By age five it is nearly fully grown. It's an organ, and organs are made up of tissue, and tissue is made up of cells. Although everything is interconnected, it's the brain cells and the connections between these cells that really make the brain work or 'do' the thinking.

Neuroscientists generally agree the brain is composed of two types of cells; neurons and neuroglia cells, and it's neurons which create our thinking and programming. We have lots of them. It is estimated there are over 100 billion, but even neuroscientists don't know for sure, and like each of us, every neuron is different and unique. The neuroglia cells are the support cells but it's the neurons which are responsible for firing signals that are the basis for our thinking.

From birth, the cells make connections with other cells which is the learning we do as a child to think, move and speak. Brain development builds on itself, cells are renewed and more cells are created, and connections link up with each other in more and more complex ways and the brain continues to evolve through our experiences, relationships, and the way we use or exercise it. As we get old, it will naturally start to shrink physically and cells deplete, but mental and physical exercise can keep it healthy and effective for longer. Like a muscle in our body, using our brain is the key to realising its potential, but only if we're using it effectively.

A baby is born with the hardware and operating system or basic programming for survival. It's unique in its make up, so will have its own capacity and operational uniqueness. It wants food, to be warm, to be safe and to be loved, because love created it and it needs that human nourishment and connection. It experiences its world through its senses and each new experience lays on top of previous experiences and memories, and it starts to create programmes in its mind such as "If I cry, I get food" or "If I touch that heater, it feels uncomfortable" or any number of early experiences as it tries to survive and be loved. The baby is learning and building programmes or patterns of thinking. It's 'doing' thinking, as it experiences and develops, while everything is based on what it has already learnt and experienced, or its memories.

Different areas of the brain are believed to be responsible for different abilities, like movement and language. They develop at different rates and are all structurally unique. The key is that brain development builds on itself in more complex ways. If a baby learns something feels good, it will pursue more of that, and it will avoid that which it learns doesn't feel good.

This processing of information, filtered by learning, is the basis of how we develop our behaviour and what we believe and value. We start to learn about consequences and trade-offs and choices. The experiences cause the building of connections in the brain which is programming being installed, and although it is in the early years that we embed many programmes that stay with us for life, we can at any time throughout our life, re-programme our connections once we become aware and know what to do. Without awareness, and the action to re-programme, we'll carry on through life operating with the foundation software that we have from childhood which may not be serving us very well as adults. So, how does this programming or 'wiring' actually work and what can you do to install new programming?

Electricity and chemicals

It might sound like it's complicated but brain science is really just about three things; electrical (brainwaves), architectural (brain structures) and chemical (neurochemicals) components, working together to create a state of mind.

Every time there is a thought, one of the brain's neurons fires an electrical pulse along an axon, which is like a 'wire'. At the end of an axon is a junction, which is a tiny gap, called a synapse and at the synapse the pulse causes the release of neurotransmitters. These are information-loaded chemicals, or chemical messengers, which then send signals to other neurons along lots of other axons. Electrical signals have to be changed to chemical signals to cross the gap, and these chemicals or neurotransmitters carry the information between the neurons by crossing the synapse. It is these chemicals or neurotransmitters which cause you to feel a certain way and which in part stimulate your energy flow.

There are hundreds of different types of neurotransmitters and no universally agreed upon way of classifying all of them, but there is a consensus on the labels we give to the most important ones. Neurotransmitters are a blend with different strengths and all are unique recipes or cocktails of chemicals that cross synapses to transmit impulses from a neuron to another cell. In other words, they're messengers carrying signals from one part of the body to another (more on this in Step 3).

You don't need to know all of the chemicals or how they blend together into their unique recipes to understand enough to change your life, but it can be helpful to have a basic understanding, especially of the ones that make us feel good, and in Step 3 we will look at some of these, such as dopamine, serotonin, adrenaline and oxytocin, and examine the way they affect how you feel and how you can control and generate these naturally within yourself.

"Everything should be made as simple as possible, but not simpler." – Albert Einstein

There are an infinite number of permutations for the signals and paths between neurons and along axons. We have a limitless capacity to think and as we'll discuss in the next Step, we have limitless capacity to feel! We truly are limitless.

In short, our thinking is electricity and chemicals working within our brain structure. We have the ability to manage and direct this electricity and these chemicals when we know how. It is managing the electrics and chemicals that is the foundation to a successful and fulfilled life. Our brain is the control centre for our nervous system and we can programme, or 'wire', this control centre to determine how we want to feel.

Your thought pathways

So, we know now that thoughts move between neurons on pathways in the brain. A common analogy when learning about thought pathways is to imagine a path across a field of long grass. The more we go across the same path, the more beaten down it gets, turning the long grass to a flat, wider and entrenched path, and so it becomes easier and quicker to cross. This is how we create pathways in our brains; the more we use the same thought path, the more we're programming and building thicker, superfast wires or neural pathways. Use the pathway and it will become beaten down, but stop using it and it will become overgrown again. This is the same whether our thoughts are helpful or unhelpful, positive or negative, and whatever we repeatedly think we become.

If I learn as a child to build repeated thinking pathways such as "Crying gets me what I want," this thinking becomes a big pathway in the brain running a pattern of "Want something? Cry to get it." If I learn that to get attention I have to 'achieve' or 'be funny', these are also thinking wires or pathways which will be created in my brain. These pathways, or patterns of thoughts, can stay with us forever unless reprogrammed, and so the question we should ask is, are the programmes we currently have serving us or limiting us?

Having a programme that uses self-pity, anger, achievement or being funny, for example, to get attention (which is really love) is going to throw up problems in life and issues around relationships and feeling fulfilled. These are just a few of the very common patterns evident all around us, but the great news is we can install new programmes anytime, once we know how. We likely just haven't paused to become aware that it's just our programming. We can take charge of our thinking electricity and chemicals to make the neural pathways that are going to work for us and the life we want.

Supercharge your programming

Repeatedly thinking the same patterns creates wires or pathways in our brain, but there are also things that exponentially thicken these wires, make stronger connections and create superfast, deeper wiring. We can incorporate these tools to supercharge our brain reprogramming.

When our thoughts have emotions attached, the pathways become deeply entrenched and reinforced. This could be through an emotionally intense experience which is positive, or it could be through a negative experience which, although we would like to forget, keeps coming back to our mind in a form of worry or regret.

When we move our body while 'doing' a thinking process, we are also wiring deeper and faster, and effectively waking up our cells. It could be a hand in the air or fist pump saying for example, 'come on' or 'yes' when something great happens. This engagement of your body and your mind is a powerful way to enhance your wiring.

If you have repeated thoughts, link emotion to these and engage your physiology, you will be building high-strength, superfast broadband, thinking patterns. The goal is to have a directed mind and focused empowering programmes.

The left and right sides of the brain are believed to be functionally different, and many scientists believe female and male brains have a different way of processing. The consensus in neuroscience is that the brain is divided into the left brain, which deals predominantly with logic, linear and sequential thinking, and the right brain, which deals with associations, abstract ideas, creativity, symbolism and emotions. The structures are all slightly different which affects the operating system capabilities and the software processing. The electrical waves and the chemicals are also all slightly different, but how neural pathways are built is the same for all of us.

"Open-minded people seek to learn by asking questions; they realize how little they know in relation to what there is to know and recognize that they might be wrong; they are thrilled to be around people who know more than they do because it represents an opportunity to learn something. Closed-minded people always tell you what they know, even if they know hardly anything. They are typically uncomfortable being around those who know a lot more than they do." – Ray Dalio

Programmed by our parents

Humans have the longest period of dependency of any animal and a lot of the programming we have is from our parents or primary carers, as they're involved in a disproportionately large part of our lives. Parental intentions are usually good, and they do their best with the programming they have, but what if their thinking isn't that evolved or isn't as relevant for us in our lives at this time as it was when they were at our stage of life?

Many of us have taken on our thinking patterns, beliefs and values from the programming our parents embedded in us as children. We then carry on through life without examining this until either we're either forced to through a big life challenge or moved through inspiration and our hunger to want to become more. As Philip Larkin wrote, "They fuck you up your mum and dad. They may not mean to, but they do". Your parents did the best they could with what they had and where they were. For most of us, most of the programming we have assimilated from them has been helpful, but when we are aware of why and how we have the programming we do, we can change it if we want to.

We can make sure our minds are working for us and the life we want, not our parents' life or the life our parents want for us. We know that we can re-programme ourselves and rewire our thinking, and we know how neurons fire up and send signals to other neurons, but how do you install this new programming most effectively for your life? Firstly, you need to decide the life you want, so you have a clear direction for your thinking, and then you need to actively direct your brain to create the wiring, the neural pathways and patterns of connections to make this happen.

What are you focusing on?

In Step 5, we'll look at the importance of having a clear philosophy for the purpose of your life, and in the final 'next steps' section we'll look specifically at all the main areas of your life so you can design your own personal action plan. The critical starting point is focus. Where focus goes energy flows, and without focus an undirected mind will jump around all over the place, creating a more complicated and frustrating life as things aren't operating efficiently. The more we focus on something, the more other thoughts to support that focus will appear in our consciousness. This is mainly because of a little system in our brain called the reticular activating system (RAS), which, in very simple terms, is a bundle of nerves at our brainstem that filters out unnecessary information so the important stuff gets through. There is so much stimuli around us it's impossible to process it all, and our brain has to filter it so we don't become an overwhelmed and confused mess. The RAS is the reason you think of buying a particular car or clothing item and then you see them everywhere.

"What we see depends mainly on what we look for." – John Lubbock

Your RAS works automatically, taking what you focus on and creating a filter for it, finding more of that to support what you are focusing on, without you noticing.

EXERCISE 10
What You Look for You See

Look around for ten seconds and find everything you can see that is green. Everything. Look for green clothes, green leaves, green grass, green cars, whatever you can see that is green.

Ok, now close your eyes and think about what you saw.

How much red did you see?

Almost certainly you will not have seen much, if any red, as you simply were not looking for it. You just saw what you were looking for.

If you now do the same exercise but this time look for red, you likely will see lots of red.

Everything is out there, it just depends what you are looking for. You see what you look for and your RAS is helping you do this filtering and focus.

Think about the world around you and examples of deception and crime. These could be something you heard about, read about or witnessed yourself. Think of the people impacted and how they were treated. Think of what seems unfair and cruel.

When you were thinking of this did you find any examples of incredible kindness and selfless giving, and did you see the impact this had on people and how they felt?

We see what we are looking for. Our mind is trying to help protect us by looking for what's wrong, but we must train ourselves to look for what's great and what's right.

What's wrong is always available, but so too is what's right.

If you are focusing on what you have, what you can control and the present, your RAS will be working to reinforce this positive empowering focus. If you're focusing on what's missing, what you can't control and the past, your RAS is going to find loads of crap to support that focus. In the same way, the RAS seeks information that validates your beliefs. It filters the world through the parameters you give it. If you think you're bad at maths, you probably will be. If you believe you are bad at public speaking, you probably will be. The RAS helps you see what you want to see and in doing so, influences your actions.

With focus and a direction, you are training your mind, and more particularly your RAS, to work for you. If you focus hard on your goals, your RAS will reveal the people, information and opportunities that will help you achieve these goals, and this is pretty much the essence of the law of attraction. Focus on the bad things and you will invite negativity into your life. Focus on the good things and they will come to you, because your brain is seeking them out. It's not magic, it's your RAS influencing the world you see around you.

"Goals are like magnets. They'll attract the things that make them come true." – *Tony Robbins*

EXERCISE 11
What Are You Focusing On?

Ask yourself these three questions:

1. Am I focusing on what I have or what is missing?
2. Am I focusing on what I can control or what is not in my control?
3. Am I focusing on the past, present or future?

Keep this as a framework to ask yourself regularly to stay focused.

Make these questions a habitual reference point to keep in check your thinking. Focusing on what you have, what you can control and on being present and planning for the future is going to make your thinking more effective and give you a much more enjoyable experience of life.

Dealing with negative patterns

A lot of thoughts people have are to do with 'bad' things that have happened in the past, or worries or fears about something that might happen in the future. These repeated thoughts are creating pathways to not feeling great, and our RAS finds things to support these negative feelings and memories. When we say to ourselves things like 'this always happens to me', or 'life isn't fair', your brain is looking for things to support those beliefs. We often create patterns that repeat these bad memories over and over. We need to break these patterns and get focusing on the good stuff. It's impossible to process everything but when you have focus, your brain is going to be more efficient.

If one of your goals is to buy a home within 12 months, and you have a clear focus, your brain will start working and looking for ways to make that happen. Focus encourages clarity and clarity precedes success, as already mentioned in Step 1. Repetition is the mother of learning, and in brain science terms this is neural pathway building. The more times we follow the same path though the wild grass, the more we beat a path which is easier and quicker to pass. If we are focused, know where we are going and repeatedly make the same thoughts, we will create powerful wiring in our brains. Sounds easy, but if we're repeating unhelpful or disempowering thoughts, we'll build wiring that will take us very efficiently to somewhere we don't want to be.

EXERCISE 12
Think of a Previous Accomplishment

Think of something you achieved that made you feel very proud. It could be anything from anytime, but ensure it's something about which you felt a great sense of achievement.

Now think about what you did to make that happen.

Did you have a clear focus about what you wanted to achieve?

Did you take repeated action in that direction?

Were you easily distracted?

Were you committed to your outcome?

In answering these questions, you will unravel the formula that you can apply for your success in any area of your life.

Linking emotion to fuel action

We can know what to do but still find it hard to change. Many people want to lose weight or get fit and they know what to do. It's simple: put fewer calories in your mouth and move more. But understanding alone is not enough to build superfast highways in your brain to create results, and we need to link emotion to understanding as it's emotion that will be the fuel to determine action.

We can link an expectation of pain or pleasure to any thoughts, and together with understanding this will be a powerful way of rewiring. If you want to change something, like eating less, and link massive pain to the consequences of eating too much, you will likely eat less. Think of the consequences if you carry on overeating; what will your life be like in one year, five years, ten years? What will it have cost you? What will you have missed out on? Is that going to make you feel good about your life? Now link massive pleasure to the future of eating better, by thinking of the consequences. What will your life be like if you feel full of energy, vibrant and radiating health? What will that enable you to do? How will you look and feel? The deeper you go into visualising and feeling the consequences, the more you will be activating your emotions and the more you will want to choose the right path. Thoughts and understanding alone will seldom be enough to effect a change in engrained behaviour patterns.

If we want to give up smoking, we know to just stop putting cigarettes between our lips but we may not have trained our minds to be successful at that process. We may be running unhelpful processes or programming. We may limit or jeopardise ourselves by the way we think and in the way we link our beliefs and emotions around our goals, whether we are conscious of that or not. We react to habitual patterns of thinking, often being consciously unaware of what we're even doing. The old software runs until we become aware and motivated to upgrade to software more effective for the life we want to create.

People usually only change when the pain of doing something becomes unbearable, and when so much emotion is stacked onto their wiring, but when we proactively take control of our thinking we can create our own rewiring by linking emotion in our minds before we get desperate. When you repeat empowering focused thoughts and now also link emotion, you are efficiently rewiring your brain for better results.

We already discussed the power of movement to help supercharge your programming, and how you can embed successful action-activating thought patterns by incorporating your body as you are repeating the thoughts and linking emotion. Physically moving can be as simple as clenching your fist or raising your arms to the sky. The combination of having directed thoughts, linking emotion and feeling it in your body as you move is the most powerful way to rewire yourself.

EXERCISE 13
Say Yes to Your Goals

Think of a clear goal and what you need to do to achieve that goal.

Now imagine you did the work and have already accomplished that goal.

Think of what it feels like and the consequences of achieving that goal. Think of how your life is different, how you have left the pain or dissatisfaction of where you were. Feel proud of the achievement and the steps you took to get there.

Now clench your fist as you imagine it done. When you clench your fist, you are locking in the destination, and programming your mind for success.

As you repeatedly clench you fist, start chanting to yourself, simply saying over and over: 'yes', 'yes', 'yes', 'yes'…

Get animated and drive your fist into the air. Move and get louder as you lock in that feeling of achieving your goal. You have done it. You are seeing, hearing and feeling your success.

Get louder and more animated: Say 'YES', 'YES', 'YES'… 'FUCK YES!'

You did it. It feels great!

Keep doing this and feel confident, proud, and alive as you imagine being in the moments of your achievement.

When you are ready, come back to the present.

You know you ***can*** and ***are*** going to make it happen. You are in control and you know in this state you can make anything happen.

You can change your emotional state at any time by changing your physiology and this is usually the best place to start. Physiology first. The body can give so much leverage to our thinking yet the body is often thought of as something separate from our brain which is seen as the computer on our shoulders. However, everything is interconnected (Step 6) and you can radically change your life by tuning into how you move.

Your whole body is you, and when you wake up all your cells, everything feels better. With this changed state, you make decisions with more clarity and speed, your relationships improve, and you become more aware, bringing alive the core you, the true essence of your humanness. In this state, you won't negotiate with yourself, you'll do what you know is right and do it without hesitation. Change your state and change your life, and you can do it quickly.

Using incantations

One of the most effective tools to put this focus, repetition, emotion and movement together to create certainty within you and build superfast empowering connections in your brain, are incantations. They are a very powerful programming tool and you can use incantations for building wires and positive thought patterns about anything. In terms of our own identity, for example, what we say to ourselves is who and what we become and powerful incantations can be used to create the identity we would like.

Begin practicing incantations starting with the words "I am…" and then what you repeatedly tell yourself following this, with emotion and using your body, will be a powerful tool in creating the new you.

You might feel awkward doing the following exercise if you're not used to practicing incantations, but trust the process; it works. Incantations are one of the most powerful ways we can start rewiring our brains and giving clear direction to our control centre. Incantations build new programs in our minds with directed thought, repetition and changes in our body cells through movement and sound. The use of language, what you focus on and how you move your body is a powerful combination for programming your mind to create and lock in new patterns for enhanced living.

EXERCISE 14
Create Your Personal Power Incantations

Find a place where you won't be disturbed and where you can shout and jump around.

Who are you? Ask yourself who is [insert your name here]? Who do you want to be? Who WILL you be?

You know the real you, the spirited you, you know what you are capable of, you know from deep inside your soul that you were born to do great things. You know wherever you have been is preparation and has given you invaluable lessons.

Start with the words "I am..." and start just randomly saying words that come to you that describe who you really are. You decide who you are, choose whatever feels right for you. You are a unique force of nature.

Here are some examples, but it can be anything you like. It's your identity.

Make a list of your own words and then start:
I am love.
I am courage.
I am joy.
I am happy.
I am free.
I am grateful.
I am powerful.
I am a force of life.
I am fucking awesome.
I am strong.
I am giving.
I am compassionate.
I am an incredible unique gift.
I am the light.
I am determined.
I am a force for good.

Now choose three of your "I am..." statements that you like best and make these your Personal Power Incantations.

Shout them loudly, get animated, make a first, punch the air, jump! If it feels weird... keep doing it! This works!

This is your life and you are the programmer. Make it a habit, do it daily. Engrain it in your mind. This is your identity and you create who you are.

I am…
I am…
I am…

The most powerful force of our behaviour is being consistent with our self-identity and we become who we tell ourselves we are. If you tell yourself "I am stupid" or "I am lazy" or "I am disorganised" or "I am bad with money", then this self-talk and self-imaging is forming your identity. You decide your identity so why not decide to be great? You can create and use incantations for anything you want to change, achieve or become. Write them down, put them on Post-it notes, and most importantly, shout them loudly with emotion and using your body. Then repeat repeat repeat!

Incantations can be anything you choose and this self-direction is programming. We're generally not taught the importance of self-talk, the importance of the quiet whispers we tell ourselves or the loudest, most animated repeated incantations. Examples of other empowering incantations include statements like:

"All I need is within me now."
"I compare myself not to others but to my previous self."
"I strive to impress myself not others."
"I never fail I either win or I learn."
"I am a force for good."
"I appreciate the perfect beauty and love that is life."
"Thank you thank you thank you."
"Life is working for me not to me."

Using uplifting language

We don't often think much about the words we use in our daily experiences, but the language we use in everything is critical to how we'll feel. If you ask someone how they're doing, common responses might include: "I'm doing pretty good" or "Not bad" or "Could be worse" or "Hanging in there" or "Getting by." Now imagine if someone said "I'm feeling awesome, thank you," "I'm on top of the world," "Unstoppable," "Excited," or "So grateful and happy!" The person who talks like this, using positive uplifting language, will have a very different physiology. Would you like to feel like that? You don't have to fake it but you can easily train yourself to feel great. The language you use whether it's power incantations or conversation is vitally important programming.

EXERCISE 15
Make More Effective Language Patterns

Decide on the language patterns you're going to use when someone asks "How are you?" or a similar greeting question. Decide to have better responses and use more empowering words.

Practise this as much as you can for the next week, and observe how you feel and how different others are around you when you have more empowering uplifting positive language patterns.

For example, phrases like "I feel great, thanks," "Feeling brilliant, thank you," and "Really good, and you?" are going to change how you, and the person asking, feel!

And when you use this language, add a smile, feel strong and calm, and see how your experience of the situation changes.

The great thing about using more empowering and uplifting language is that not only will you feel more empowered and uplifted yourself, so will those you interact with, and your words will have an impact far beyond what you can likely imagine (more in Step 6). Who would you feel better meeting; the person with sluggish attitude, dropped shoulders and low energy who says "Not too bad, am getting by" or the person alive with energy, great posture and a smile who says "Really great, thank you." Of course, some people have physical pain to deal with and this is not all about fake smiles and pretending everything is amazing, but if you focus on the language you use, you can change how you and others feel. Even when crap is happening, you can rise above it and use empowering language to stop falling into self-pity and disempowering physiology.

Encourage yourself and keep it fun

The language we use is critically important and nowhere more so than how we talk to ourselves. We all have internal dialogue and how we talk to ourselves will determine how we feel about ourselves. We all make mistakes, we're all learning on our journey through life on earth, and we all have things happen which we cannot control. But what we can control is how we talk to ourselves. It seems incredible to hear people berating themselves when they make a mistake, or telling themselves they aren't good at something. Telling yourself "I can't believe I did that" or "I screwed up, I'm useless" is what you will believe.

From this moment on, think of talking to yourself as how you would talk to a child. How would a child feel if you berated them for falling over when they were learning to walk? Or for making a mistake while learning? You wouldn't be helping the child progress very well. Giving a child clear instructions, lots of encouragement and keeping it fun will be much more successful. Give yourself clear instructions, lots of encouragement, and keep it fun and you will transform your own life. Become acutely aware of how you are talking to yourself and if you catch yourself using unhelpful language, just encourage yourself and keep it fun. You are human and humans learn by making mistakes.

EXERCISE 16
Improve How You Talk to Yourself

Start becoming more aware of how you talk to yourself in the following situations:

1. When things haven't gone your way.
   Every time you catch yourself saying something disempowering, make a flicking action (discretely if you need to) with your fingers of your dominant hand. This is to signify you have noticed how unhelpful your self-chat is (which is great awareness) and that you're flicking it away; you know negative self-talk is rubbish, and needs to be disposed of.

2. When you have a goal and you are making progress towards it.
   In these situations, every time you catch yourself saying something encouraging or uplifting, clench your fist or pinch your thumb and forefinger. This is again to appreciate how aware you are of your self-talk, but knowing this time you are being helpful to yourself and having empowering thoughts. Lock these feelings in by creating what we call an anchor, which is just a reminder of the feeling and a trigger (fist clench) you can use to activate that feeling anytime you choose.

The more you practise this the more aware you will become of how you are talking to yourself and the more you will be able to flick away rubbish self-talk and encourage positive chat habitually.

How you talk to yourself, your internal dialogue, is building neural pathways. You are the builder, the electrician of your brain, and this is your life, so make sure you are building the most helpful pathways you can.

How you talk to yourself is critical and so too is how you see yourself. We are all making pictures and movies in our minds all the time, and our task is to become great film producers and manage the picture making we are doing so it works in the best way possible for us.

EXERCISE 17
Understand the Power of Your Imagination

Close your eyes and imagine you are walking in the blistering dry heat of the desert. You're feeling parched, your mouth is dry and you are dehydrated.

Now imagine holding a chilled, juicy lemon and gently squeezing that into your mouth. Feel the cool liquid dropping onto your tongue as it keeps coming and coming.

Open your eyes. How did that make your mouth feel? Your mouth will almost certainly be watering and although this is just a simple example, it shows the power of your imagination to make physical changes. You have only used your imagination, it's not real, and yet your body responds as if it was.

The power of visualisation

As humans, we have an incredible capacity to imagine but our minds don't know the difference between real and imagined. Visualisation is one of the most effective tools in training and although 'film-making in the mind' has been a training focus in high level sport, it's now becoming much more accepted as a mainstream performance tool. There was a piece of research with basketball players in the US where some players practiced free throws and some just imagined or visualised making the free throws over and over again. When it came to then taking free throws against each other, the players who had used just visualisation performed best. In every visualisation or practice they were seeing the shot perfectly each time.

How you are making pictures in your mind affects how you see yourself and what you do. *Your self-image is created by you.* We burden ourselves by thinking about what others might be thinking of us but we create who we are and we can't control pictures and films others are making of us. If you have a less-than-amazing self-image, you're making a picture in your head of a less-than-amazing person. Instead, work on creating pictures in your mind of the great person you are.

If you're feeling anxious about something (which is really just 'doing' anxious thoughts), for example maybe thinking about going into a room full of strangers and getting nervous, then you're making a movie in your head of what you imagine will happen, and it's not a very pleasant movie to watch. If you're doing anxious thoughts ahead of the event, it's all made up anyway because you haven't gone into the room yet! It's your imagination and so you need to make better movies that are going to make you feel better. Changing the movie you are playing in your mind will change how you feel which will change what you do.

EXERCISE 18
Visualising the Real Confident You

Before you go to a party, an office meeting or a gathering of strangers, pause and just for a few moments imagine there is a version of you, standing just in front.

That person is compassionate, kind, funny and warm and someone people really like and want to connect with. This person is totally at ease with the situation and has a lightness and warmth that radiates. They have real presence and self-assuredness.

Now imagine stepping forward and into that person. As you step into this version of you, feel what it feels like to be so cool, calm and collected. See what they see, hear what they hear in that environment and feel what they feel, ready to enjoy meeting others.

This is you, this is the real person you are. You know people really want to talk with that sort of person. They are drawn to the confidence and lightness.

Now smile and enter the room with confidence and grace. Your presence speaks loudly before you have even said a word.

Visualisation is one of the most powerful techniques in mastering your mind and creating your best life. Everything is essentially created twice. First in your mind and then in your life. If you want to do anything, you first create a movie of it in your mind and so how you create this movie is incredibly important. We need to become great film producers in our minds and direct effective pictures. We are visualising anyway, whether we are conscious of this or not, so we may as well visualise for what we want and who we will become. Practise visualising and you will get better at it. See the goal and outcome clearly and then see yourself in that visualisation of success. First, make it real in your mind and then you make it real in reality, like the basketball players in the earlier example who first saw perfect outcomes in their mind. Successful people are not playing movies in their mind of things not working out, they're making movies of what they want to happen. They are great film producers.

It would be great to see visualisation being taught more widely in schools as it is an invaluable technique we should be teaching to all our children. They have great imaginations anyway, so think of the benefits if they started at an early age regularly using imagination in a directed way like this. Some schools already include this more than others, but we advocate visualisation being elevated as a core part of the curriculum for every child.

EXERCISE 19
Visualise a Goal Achieved

Think of one of your main goals in life.

Now imagine that you have already achieved it in the same way you did in Exercise 13.

That exercise was primarily to engage your physiology, and this exercise is primarily to practise visualisation.

Be in that moment when the work is done, when you have realised the outcome, when you are right there at the place of victory, and success.

See yourself in all the detail exactly as it will be when you have achieved this goal.

What does it feel like?
What can you see?
What can you hear?

Imagine being in this film running in your mind, this movie of the success you have achieved.

Now as you see yourself there, and it feels great and satisfying, imagine turning up all the feelings you have. Imagine everything you see is more vivid, everything you are hearing is so clear, it feels fantastic and satisfying. Well done. You did it and it feels awesome!

Now, as we did in Exercise 13, clench your fist as you're feeling so intensely your success, and as you do that you will lock in that vision of achieving your goal.

Clenching your fist anchors in the feeling, and gives your unconscious mind a clear target which you can now move towards without resistance.

Try it – this thinking 'technology' is really effective. You already know that the unconscious mind doesn't know the difference between what's real and what's imagined, so if you are imagining your future you may as well imagine a fantastic one, and then move there.

Create your vision board

Practice visualisation, incorporate this technique into your life and you will change how you feel and what you do. Seeing it done first and then creating it in your life is giving your powerful unconscious mind the directions it needs.

A powerful tool for creating the life you want is to create for yourself a physical vision board, or a physical representation of the life you want, bringing together in visual form all your goals. You can keep this somewhere you will see it regularly and update it as you need. You will be giving your mind focus and your RAS instructions on what to filter. By seeing your vision board regularly, you are reinforcing your neural pathways through repetition.

EXERCISE 20
Create Your Vision Board

Get a large board or piece of clean white card, big enough that you can put lots of images and notes on. Let's call this your Vision Board.

Now spend some time collating, from whatever sources you choose, images that represent the life you want so you can see the future you are going to create. Make it clear in terms of the specific areas rather than just a dump of pictures. Magazine content, photographs, internet images, or whatever you can find that visually represents areas of your future life which you are going to make real.

For example, you can have images that represent your health and fitness goals, what your financial freedom will look like, places you will travel to, spiritual growth, relationships, family, charitable goals. It's your life and your vision board, so make it excite and inspire you.

Add words, draw pictures or whatever you decide will be a helpful visual representation. The more inspiring your vision board, the more it will create clarity for your unconscious mind and your RAS.

See it first and then your mind will be working for you even when you're not consciously thinking or being aware of this.

When you have completed your vision board, place it somewhere you will see it regularly. This will remind you, excite you and further trigger your unconscious mind to work efficiently for you.

Replacing unhelpful pictures

Creating effective pictures in your mind is one of the most powerful skills you can develop and the better you get at this, the better your life will be. If you make unhelpful pictures, you'll likely have an unpleasant experience. People get anxious by creating or imagining unhelpful pictures, but we can change the pictures and change our feelings, as we did with the exercise on building confidence before entering a room full of strangers. You can also give yourself more space to create effective pictures, by clearing away some of the old negative ones.

When you visualise, if you are making films or recalling memories that you don't like, imagine yourself stepping out of the film and observing it. It happened in the past so you're able to just be an observer. Once you're outside the film, you can do what you like with the pictures. You can pause, rewind, scramble, dull the colour, mute the sound and push it far away or just dissolve the redundant film you don't like. When the film is one you really like, you can stay in the film and feel, see and hear as vividly as you can, amplifying all the sensory inputs. This simple technique of immersing yourself in movies you like and extracting yourself and changing films you don't is a useful technique in your armoury of tools for managing your mental imagery and storage.

EXERCISE 21
Wash Your Mind

Is there something that happened in the past that you spend a lot for time thinking about and which doesn't make you feel good? Most people have something, or lots of things!

How much of your life is spent thinking about this? How much time are thoughts about this eating up daily? Weekly? Monthly? Even a couple of hours a day can end up at over 30 days every year just thinking about this thing!

How would you like a month of your life back every year? What could you do with that time?

When you think about the event/person that is distressing, you are effectively watching a film of this in your mind. The event has passed, the person isn't here, so all you are doing is imagining or watching the movie which is unhelpful, and probably distorted.

Now think about this film you are watching. Where is that film playing? What size is it? Is it moving? Is it in colour?

When we focus on past events that are making us not feel great, usually we are seeing a big moving film, close up, in colour and with sounds. It is very real in your mind as it's causing you to feel so crap.

So, as you think about the event that causes you to think distressing thoughts, watch the movie and then imagine condensing it into a bundle of pictures or a video file. Now take that compressed file and move it further away, shrink it down, drain all the colour and sound out of it and now zap it away in a puff of smoke with a click of your fingers.

It may seem strange if you're not used to doing this, but keep practising and you'll become much more aware of these films playing in your mind and you'll find it easy to use the technique of getting rid of unhelpful, time-eating memories.

You will be rinsing your mind of redundant storage.

You are the film producer and director, even if you hadn't thought of it that way before.

Become more aware of the movies you are watching, get rid of the crap ones and make great new ones. It's as simple as that.

Understanding your unconscious mind

The terms brain and mind are often used interchangeably, but they are different. The brain is a physical organ, a processor. It's our hardware, we know exactly where it's located and we understand a lot about its physical properties. The mind, however, includes the output of the brain's activities, and is invisible within us, including our thoughts, beliefs, self-talk and imagination, and while it has been usual to think of the mind as being just in the brain, our mind is really within our whole body. It's in every cell of who we are.

We process information from the world around us through our senses in images, sounds, smells, tastes and feelings, and we represent this processed information internally. There is a lot of stimuli so the brain works to generalise, delete and distort based on what we have already experienced. It would be impossible to process everything so we have to filter. When we're thinking, we're primarily creating pictures and sounds and recalling memories or using our imagination, but because of the volume and complexity of information to process, and functions to manage, our mind operates on two levels: The conscious level which we are aware of, and a level below the surface which we are not consciously aware of; our unconscious.

The conscious mind is easy to understand and you are using it now to read this. It's able to deal with up to nine ideas or experiences at any one time. The unconscious mind, however, is limitless. Everything we have ever seen, heard, smelled, tasted and felt are stored in our unconscious mind. It also stores patterns of programming or learning which enable us to do a lot of things without being consciously aware.

When we learn a new skill like riding a bike or driving a car, we first learn with our conscious mind and then the learning goes into our unconscious mind so we can perform without consciously being aware. The unconscious mind also controls our heartbeat, breathing and many other functions that run the human body. We would otherwise be completely overwhelmed and it would be impossible to be conscious of everything, so our unconscious mind runs most of what is going on. For example, when the information about driving is stored in your unconscious mind, it is stored like software that can be run automatically whenever needed. It's your autopilot.

EXERCISE 22
Build Awareness of Your Unconscious Mind

Wherever you are reading this, just for a moment touch your nose with your right hand.
Ok, now relax. That was very simple, wasn't it?

You likely did this very easily and quickly but can you explain what had to happen to do that? It's quite a remarkable sequence of actions involving muscles, ligaments, feelings and memory just to do something like that very simple task, but your unconscious mind did this easily for you. You didn't have to consciously think about what to do. Your unconscious mind already had the programming installed.

You could do any amount of other body moving actions and of various complexity, but hopefully you've already understood just from this simple example, that your unconscious mind is your autopilot working for you based on the programming, or instructions you have already installed.

Whether it's walking, riding a bicycle, or skiing, these are all very complex physical actions, but once you've learnt them, you can do them without much conscious awareness.

Our conscious mind learns by logic and repetition and our unconscious mind stores and takes direction and suggestion, being most receptive when it's in a relaxed state. It is easier to programme when the mind isn't distracted by external stimulus. The patterns of programming which our unconscious mind is already running can be very helpful, but there are also patterns of programming which may not be helping us, especially in areas of belief, values and habits. If, for example, you really want to be in a great fulfilling relationship, but your unconscious mind is programmed to do 'scared of commitment', then you'll unconsciously be looking for people you don't have to commit to. You may have built an unconscious wall to protect yourself, but that wall will also be imprisoning you. Or if you believe all the best people have been taken, then you'll be unconsciously looking for 'what's wrong' with everyone you meet.

Quieting the mind

We need to create new programmes for our unconscious mind to replace the unhelpful or limiting ones and align our conscious thoughts with our unconscious ones to give a clear direction. Meditation, mindfulness and hypnosis are all great practices to help us manage our mind and all of these are about quieting the mind and lessening external stimulation so the brain can focus with direction. Don't worry too much about the labels; these aren't important. What is important is that they are all tools to quieten the mind.

When we put our mind into a less distracted state, it's much more susceptible to suggestions and taking instructions. Hypnosis may seem daunting to some, but it is really just the same mind-quieting process as meditation and mindfulness, but with the aim to focus and change, rather than just being aware of our thoughts. These mind-quieting practices have been going on as long as people have been sitting calmly with their eyes shut, but now the benefits of meditation, mindfulness and hypnosis are increasingly science-backed. It's quite a simple idea to understand that a quieter, more focused mind, that's looking inside rather than out, is going to be more efficient and open than a busy distracted mind.

"Everyone should meditate for 20 minutes a day. If you are too busy you should meditate for an hour." – old Zen saying

EXERCISE 23
Quieten Your Mind

Sit comfortably and quietly and when you are relaxed just bring your attention to your breathing.

Breathe in deeply and exhale slowly, noticing every breath. Keep breathing in and out, slow deep breaths from the diaphragm.

Now let your mind just wander, and as you do, it will have lots of thoughts. That's how it operates, it generates thoughts, it runs patterns and processes. Observe these thoughts, but keep returning to your breath.

Enjoy feeling calm and relaxed, with each breath out releasing all tensions and stress from your body, and with each inhale bringing fresh, new, energised oxygen to your body.

You're already experiencing having more mind control, as when you focus on your breathing you can't also be aware of having other thoughts at the same time. When you take your focus away from your breathing however, you'll become aware of your thoughts again.

Focus again on your breathing and just quietly say "Thank you" with each exhale. You don't need to be conscious of being thankful for anything in particular, just repeat as you breathe out; "Thank you," "Thank you," "Thank you"...

This is a very simple example of a quieting mind exercise and there are many ways you can practice mind calming. The essence is to keep returning to your breath, know you have control of what you focus on, and that your thoughts are just thoughts.

Our limiting beliefs

We often know what we *want* to do, but we have invisible blocks such as limiting beliefs, values and habits which are reinforced unconscious patterns that cause unhelpful thoughts and feelings that stop us taking effective action. This unconscious programming drives how you feel and what you do. I can know what to do but I need my conscious and unconscious to be aligned if I am going to take the action necessary to change. Beliefs are the lenses through which you interpret the world and your experiences, and they colour everything you say and think. They are just reinforced patterns in your brain mostly based on memories and experiences.

We aren't born with any beliefs, we form them. Beliefs are the neural pathways which have become entrenched, and which we believe with certainty based on our experiences and programming from our environment. These beliefs, and entrenched pathways, often remain unexamined through people's lives and one of the biggest problems is that people don't realise their beliefs are only beliefs. If we were taught this from an early age, there likely would be a lot less conflict and war in the world. It's important to be aware of our beliefs and ask whether they are limiting or disempowering us in pursuit of the life we want. If they are limiting us, we need to destroy them and replace them with empowering ones. We all have some beliefs that limit us and these are usually, to some degree, thinking we're not enough in some area of life such as "I'm not young enough," "Not old enough," "Not smart enough," "Not attractive enough," "Not educated enough," "Not rich enough."

At their core, limiting beliefs are about our deepest fear, which is that we aren't enough, and if we aren't enough, that we won't be loved. However, if we're aware of these unhelpful beliefs which are blocking us, we can crush them and replace them with new, empowering beliefs and unleash our limitless power.

"Our life is the creation of our mind." – Buddha

We already know from earlier in the chapter that to make new, superfast 'broadband' pathways, we need to link emotion and movement to wire this into our bodies. To crush a limiting belief, we need to replace the old unhelpful belief with a new empowering one, which is usually the opposite, and build a superfast pathway to it.

EXERCISE 24
Crush Your Limiting Beliefs

Read this exercise. Then re-read it. Make sure you really understand the instructions before you start.

When you're ready, think of a belief you have that's limiting you. (We all have some of these, so don't kid yourself and pretend you don't have any!) Focus now on this limiting belief you have chosen, and as you think of it, close your eyes and imagine what it would it be like to hang onto this belief as you carry on through life.

Think of the pain it will cause, what you'll miss out on in life, who you'll miss, and the effect it will have on those around you.

The impact would likely be huge. Go deep and imagine the 'cost' to your life in five years. Think about what your life would look like if you still had that limiting belief after all that time. How would that feel?

Now go further, to ten years in your future with the same beliefs, and what it would cost you in a decade.

Keep going, for another ten years, that's 20 years from now. What is your life going to be like in 20 years if you hang onto this, and other, bullshit limiting beliefs? That's 20 years of limiting your life because of a belief you have installed as software in your mind?

The more vividly and intensely you imagine being in the future with this limiting belief, the more effective the exercise will be, as your body, mind, and soul really need to associate the pain that will be caused by living with the same old bullshit belief.

Can you change? Can you get out of that pain? You must decide, and if you have done the exercise correctly you will be in no doubt that you cannot hold onto that limiting belief any longer, that belief which will cause so much pain for the rest of your life.

When you've reached a point of imagining the pain as so unbearable, decide to say NO, this is bullshit. Tell yourself you don't want that pain, you refuse to accept the pain and the damage. You can change and you will change and you will change now!

Having decided to eliminate this unhelpful blocking belief, now all you need to do is install a new empowering belief in place of the now crushed limiting one.

With the new empowering belief, now imagine yourself in five, ten and 20 years and what your life will look like with this new belief. How will you feel? Who will be in your life? How different will your life be?

Once you have installed the new belief, you can revisit your old limiting belief and laugh at the absurdity of the old crap programming you were holding on to. You can shout as an incantation your new belief in its place, if that helps you, but either way you know you have reprogrammed yourself and your unconscious mind is unlocked.

You decide what you believe, you control your life and you create your future. Being aware of what is holding you back, what unhelpful beliefs you've been holding onto and knowing how to change these, is a huge part of your personal growth.

Identify your values

Based on what we believe and our experiences in life, we all learn that there are some feelings or emotional states we value more than others. There are feelings that we want to have more of in our lives and feelings we want to experience less of, or move away from. These are our values and alongside our beliefs they are our guiding force for everything we do, but are we aware of these and whether they are working for the life we want? Your values are a hidden force driving you, but are they congruent?

We all want to move towards certain values and away from others but often there's a conflict. For example, can you be really successful and liked by everyone? The idea is to understand your values, or what's important to you. Your brain works to put things in a hierarchy so whether we are aware or not, we have values and we prioritise them. We have probably never stopped to study our values, but when we become more aware, we can consciously choose the values we want in the hierarchy we want and we can make sure there are no conflicts. Once we have done this, we can then make superhighway neural pathways to these feel good values, and narrow or erase the pathways to values we want to avoid.

EXERCISE 25
Assess Your Values

Start with a clean sheet of paper and draw a line down the middle.

What's really important to you? What feelings are you really trying to pursue and what makes you feel that way?

On the left side of the line make a list of all these emotional states that you value most in life. They could be, for example: freedom, justice, growth, joy, vitality… write down anything you feel you want to write down. Don't get too bogged down, just write what flows instinctively. Five or six words is enough.

When you have finished making this list, make another list on the right side of everything you are trying to avoid or don't like in terms of your feelings. This could include, for example (but remember these are your own very personal values that you must decide are true for you): injustice, frustration, anger, jealousy, envy…

We're not trying to make an exhaustive list, so just write down what comes to you.

Now you should have two lists. Label them, simply as your 'towards values' on the left and your 'away from values' on the right.

You can refine these lists and the values as you grow at any time, but the key is to be ***aware*** of your top values which are steering your life, and most importantly to examine if any are potentially conflicting.

If your top values are, for example, adventure but also security, you will have an inbuilt conflict in your operational programming.

Bringing your values into your consciousness, examining them and working to rearrange them to work for you in alignment, is a critical part of realising your potential and feeling really fulfilled in life. This is what the exercise is all about.

Become more aware of your values and understand the order in which you are prioritising them.

You are in the director's chair and you now can organise your values to propel yourself forward rather than feel conflicted or blocked.

All success starts in your mind and you have all the tools in this chapter, Step 2, of the SYSO System, to become your own great neuro manager. Be the director of your mind, control how you think and you can change your life. Install better programmes. You have learnt some great mind-management exercises in this Step and like all exercises, you need to commit to repeating these and practising. You don't become fit and strong by going to the gym only once; the training, and growing, never stops.

"Nourish the mind like you would your body. The mind cannot survive on junk food." – *Brian Tracy*

STEP 3
Take Charge of Your Emotions

"You cannot always control what goes on outside, but you can always control what goes on inside." – Wayne Dyer

The quality of your life really boils down to how you feel emotionally. This is the flavouring of your experiences. You could be a billionaire and yet often feel frustrated, angry, guilty, envious, bitter and full of regrets or you could be stone-cold broke but feel inspired, excited about the future, grateful and full of laughter and love for life. Which would you rather be?

Well the good news is you don't have to choose, as life can offer both financial freedom and happiness. It's not an either/or game between areas of achievement and fulfilment, even if it might seem like that sometimes. Although we strive to achieve things like money, great relationships, optimum health or a great job, it's really just the feelings these things give us which we are seeking.

We tend to be striving for things outside ourselves, but it's really our internal world which will determine how we feel. Working on our internal world is the key to living our best life. The world is full of examples of miserable wealthy people and very happy poor people, and happiness and fulfilment isn't tied to either financial position; it's tied to the internal world of your emotion and primarily your most usual go-to emotional states. Having more money will just magnify the kind of person you are anyway. If you're a beautiful, compassionate and generous soul who values the impact your life has on other lives, being wealthy will make you more of that person, and if you are doing selfish, intolerant and judgemental behaviour, you will likely just then be a rich version of that type of behaviour.

When you work on your own personal development and mastering emotion, you can be rich in life whatever your financial position. Happiness is not dictated by circumstances, it is (as you now know from Step 2) electric and chemical reactions within you and you can manage your own electricity and chemicals to choose exactly how you would like to feel anytime. Let's repeat that. You can choose exactly how you would like to feel anytime! If you take nothing else from the SYSO System, please take this; take responsibility for how you feel and know you always have the choice to decide how you would like to feel.

The vast majority of people seeking personal development help usually start by stating they're not happy in at least one of the following three areas of their lives; financial, relationships and fitness. They often feel that in pursuing one area of life, usually work/finance, they have neglected another like relationships or health, which may be the case, but it doesn't have to be like this. You can have abundance and success in all areas of your life but to do so you must be able to master and take charge of your emotions. It's the quality of your emotions that will determine what you do and the quality of your life, no matter where you are in your unique living journey. Crap will happen, circumstances outside of your control will be challenging, but how you react emotionally will determine how you feel. Anyone can react well when things are going well, and so it's how you deal with the bad stuff that is the most important part. It's the quality of your emotion on a consistent basis that is really the quality of your life, and managing your inner self through the days, weeks, months, years, as life changes, is how you create an outstanding existence. Once you learn how to take charge, and commit to being the manager of your self, you can decide the emotions you want to feel more of and those you want to avoid.

"When pain, misery or anger happens. It is time to look within you, not around you." – Sadhguru

What is emotion?

So, what is this thing we call emotion anyway and where does it come from? Most psychologists, therapists and self-help programs use long lists of words to describe different defined emotions that they believe exist inside us such as anger, grief, disgust, joy, sadness, apathy, shock, guilt, jealousy, shame, envy, remorse and sadness, amongst many others. Some believe there are a small number of core emotions and that all other emotions derive from these. Others focus their explanations on a belief that there are different emotions which mix together in the same way an artist mixes primary colours to create other colours.

The psychologist Robert Plutchik proposed eight basic primary emotions: fear, anger, sadness, joy, disgust, anticipation, surprise and trust, from which all other emotions arise. From these eight core emotions, he suggested there are as many as 34,000 distinguishable emotions when you consider all the different combinations and intensities! Others have suggested there are six core emotions and more recently it has been claimed that there are just four biologically basic emotions: anger, fear, happiness and sadness, on top of which have evolved much more complex varieties of emotion over time. These approaches don't suggest that emotions are any less complex, just that the basic building blocks are relatively few.

Dacher Keltner suggests there are at least 27 distinct emotions which are all intimately connected with each other. In contrast to the notion that each emotional state is a distinct separate kind of island, he believes that: *"There are smooth gradients of emotion between, say, awe and peacefulness, horror and sadness, and amusement and adoration. Everything is interconnected, much richer and more nuanced than previously thought in this approach."* Even though this accepts it is not just as simple as there being islands of different emotions, all these theories still assert that emotions, whether 4, 6, 8, 27 or 34,000, all exist within all of us all the time, just waiting to be triggered. The message with these approaches is usually about becoming more aware of these different emotions and labelling them so we can identify when they are triggered.

My question with this approach is how can we know which one is which? When something doesn't go the way I would like, am I experiencing anger or frustration or disappointment, or is it a mix of all these? No matter how many labels there are, it could be quite stressful just trying to work out which is which! And does it matter anyway?

When we think of emotions as separate, defined, specific feelings inside us, the number of emotions we can have is limited surely only by the number of different words we can come up with to describe any small difference in feeling? Not only will this list of descriptive words be infinitely large due to the variations in each person's experience of being, but other cultures and languages have terms for emotions that don't even exist in our English language. My favourite of these is the German word *Backpfeifengesicht* meaning a face badly in need of a slap! *Forelsket* is Norwegian for the electric feeling someone experiences at the start of falling in love, and *Tarab*, in Arabic, is a musically induced state of ecstasy or enchantment. *Shinrin-yoku* in Japanese means the relaxation gained from bathing in the forest, *Dadirri* is an Australian aboriginal term for a deep, spiritual act of reflective and respectful listening, and *Pihentagyú* is the literal word in Hungarian which means with a relaxed brain, while *Desenrascanço* in Portuguese, means to artfully disentangle oneself from a troublesome situation. Perhaps the simplest, and one we should pay most attention to striving for, is *Sukha* which in Sanskrit means a genuine lasting happiness independent of circumstances.

Psychologists, on top of labelling distinguishable different emotions which they believe exist within us, also like to categorise these different emotions as either positive or negative. If I'm going to master my emotions using these theories, this would mean I not only have to define and label everything I feel, but on top of that, I need to classify each emotion as positive or negative. Even if we do subscribe to the theory that there are different distinguishable emotions, can each really be classified as either negative or positive? It's how these emotions are working for us which would determine whether something is helpful or unhelpful rather than the emotion itself. It would be situational, with for example anger, frustration and fear potentially being really helpful to us in the right situation.

If I was walking home alone down a dark alley and I suddenly noticed a group of people shouting and armed with knives, would a feeling of fear be helpful to me? Of course it would. My body would go into a more alert state and I would decide to get away from there as soon as possible. If I was getting frustrated because something didn't feel right in my relationship or business, could this be a helpful signal that something needs to be changed and is a cue for action? Feelings inside us are signals, so listening to how we feel is invaluable for our growth, and developing a higher awareness of this internal world of emotion is at the heart of effective personal development.

Although there is some great and well-intentioned academic work in this area, classifying emotions as defined parcels within us may not be the most helpful way to think about our internal world of feeling, and how we can take charge of this.

Energy in motion

The SYSO System suggests looking at emotion in a different way. What if we don't have emotions waiting within us to be triggered? What if we don't actually have distinct separate emotions within us at all? What if we just have energy that is in motion which is actually the origin of the word E-motion? Rather than having lots of different emotions within us, we have electricity and chemicals which get activated to cause a feeling. We think thoughts, that cause chemicals to be released in our bodies, and electrical movements of energy within us, which together is our feeling.

We don't have anger within us, we have angry thoughts that release chemicals which change how we feel and which stimulate our electricity or energy flow, which creates a particular feeling. We can have joyful thoughts that release chemicals which stimulate our energy flow in a different way and which causes a different feeling. We can have any feeling we choose as we decide the label we put on that feeling. Every time you believe you are triggering a particular emotion, think instead about energy moving within you rather than it being a specific labelled emotion which has just been activated.

As you will see in more detail in Step 7, we are all just energy. Life is energy and we know from Step 2 that our brain processing is basically just electricity and chemicals, and chemicals can cause various chemical reactions to create further energy. Life is energy flowing, and it flows in waves.

Life energy

Have you ever seen a dead body? If you have you will know first-hand that the dead person's body is, of course, still there after they have been pronounced dead. You can see them and touch them, but life has gone from their body, and they have stopped 'being'. Their life force or energy is no longer there, it is just a body, albeit a decomposing one. The energy, or life force, within us is what makes us alive and it is moving and changing at all times, like the ocean. Everything in life is moving to some degree and *how* this life force of energy is moving within us might be a more helpful way to think about emotion. The energy moving within us primarily moves depending on the thoughts we have and the chemicals that are released as a result of those thoughts.

"An emotion is your body's reaction to your mind." – Eckhart Tolle

EXERCISE 26
Take Charge of Your Energy in Motion

1. Consider for a moment something in your life that when you think about it you have angry thoughts. It could be a breach of trust, an injustice or where you were taken advantage of.

   Whatever it is, think about it really intensely now, as if you are right there in the moment when this happened. As you think about it, become more aware of how it makes you feel. Really think about the feelings you are experiencing.

   Does it feel like there is movement within your body, is there an intensity you feel somewhere as you think about it? There will be a response in your body somehow, you just have to start being more aware of what, and where, this is.

   Each of us will experience the intensity differently but mostly it will likely be a rising feeling or a deep feeling in our gut or chest area like waves or a strong flow of energy spinning.

   Your energy has been activated to move within you in a certain way (electricity) by your thoughts and the neurotransmitters (chemicals) depending on how you were thinking about the event/person/happening and the meaning you've attached to it.

2. Now think about which way this energy flow is moving or rising in your body. All energy is moving, even if you are not aware of it. If this is your first time doing this exercise it might seem hard to really tune into how these feelings or energy flows are happening within you, but the more you do this, the more aware you will become.

3. As you feel it, now decide you are going to move it the other way, or spin it in the opposite direction. You are in charge of this energy and how it moves. It can be helpful to start using your hands to signal the movement and new direction you want, along with your thoughts instructing how you want it to flow.

4. As you are changing the energy flow, be grateful for the experience. Whatever you were thinking about that caused you to do angry thinking, and to have anger induced energy responses, you will be learning something from even if you can't see that now.

If you have followed the instructions correctly, you'll be feeling different from when you started the exercise. You will have consciously taken charge of, and changed, the way the energy moves within you and it will also feel less intense. You have taken charge of your electricity flow. It has to flow somewhere so why not take charge?

If we scanned your body as you were having your angry thoughts, we would actually see a map of different energy intensity in different parts of your body, which would show as heat for higher intensities and colder for lower intensities. We don't need to do that however, as we can build our own awareness of the movement and location of this energy within us once we start tuning into these feelings. It should be no surprise by now that it all starts with awareness.

"I don't want to be at the mercy of my emotions, I want to use them, to enjoy them, and to dominate them." – Oscar Wilde

What you have experienced in the exercise is simply being conscious of the energy within you, the energy in motion and how you can control it's flows with your thinking. This energy is the same life force that is always within you, it just moves or gets stirred up in different ways and in different intensities depending primarily on the thoughts you have and the chemicals those thoughts release. The principle is the same for all your thoughts and the energy will flow depending on the intensity of how much you like or dislike what you are thinking about. Very angry, frustrated, disappointed, envious or shocked thoughts will cause a strong flow of energy and all the flows will be completely unique depending on your thoughts.

Think of how the sea is always moving but with different force and intensity as it's either stirred or calm to varying degrees. Every flow of the sea is different; every storm, every wave and every break of water against the shoreline is unique.

Your ocean of emotion

Your emotion within you is like the ocean, and you can decide and take charge of how you want that energy flow to be moving. You can become aware of your ocean of emotion rising or subsiding. You can feel it within you moving and you can choose to either fan it and stir it up more, by continuing with more similar thoughts, or to control it.

Imagine you're floating in the ocean and the water stirs with a storm and the waves get wild. The water moves fast, and smashes against the shoreline. On the other hand, imagine the calm rocking of the water and the waves gently lapping on the shoreline. Imagine something quite dramatic happens in your life that you didn't want to happen. If you're aware and in charge, you can feel the energy in motion building and if you decide to change your thoughts and take charge, you can control your ocean of emotion, you can prevent the wild seas from causing havoc.

You can't control the events but you can control the weather patterns because these are controlled by your thinking. The question is: What kind of weather would you like? Two people can experience the same event, but if one person thinks of it is as really bad and negative, while another thinks of it as actually quite positive, their thoughts, and intensity of those thoughts, will be very different and will determine how their energy moves.

Imagine there is a car crash. One person could think this is a disaster, "It has ruined my day, I'm going to be late, why me?" while another person could be thinking "How lucky, I am so glad it wasn't worse, nobody got hurt, I have insurance which will take care of everything." The energy flow and the chemicals released by these two very different meanings and thought processes about the same event are clearly going to be very different and the experience will feel very different. One will be more intense and wild and the other much calmer.

"It's not the load that breaks you down, it's the way you carry it." – Lou Holtz

EXERCISE 27
Practise Recognising That It Always Could Be Worse

When something 'bad' happens, make the very first thing you always say be: *"It could be worse."*

It always could be worse and it is usually easy to think of worse scenarios.

By thinking it could be worse you're actually practising gratitude albeit indirectly, as you're being grateful it isn't worse!

Some things won't go your way in life, that's a certain, so it would seem smart to have effective techniques to deal with such situations. Make 'it could be worse' thinking, a habit.

If you practise this, it will become the new programming in your unconscious mind as the go-to thought pattern when anything happens that you didn't want.

Practise gratitude

One of the most powerful thinking tools you have available to you at all times is gratitude, which alone is one of the quickest ways to change how you stir emotion within you. When you have grateful thoughts, you'll be unable to think of anything negative at the same time. Try it? You can't be angry when you're being grateful. You can't feel frustrated when you're being grateful. Gratitude is your number one tool for taking charge of your emotions or changing the energy flow within you. Practise gratitude and not only will you feel differently, the more you practise, the more you'll realise there's a lot be grateful for!

EXERCISE 28
Bedtime Gratitude

Before you go to sleep, end your day with a review of how it was, and focus on gratitude.

You can do this in bed or before going to bed, but the key is to be quiet and undistracted.

Think of three things you did today which you can be particularly grateful for.

Ask yourself how you manged your emotions throughout your day and mark this on a scale of 1–10: 1 being completely out of control and 10 being totally in control. For any instances in the day where you didn't control your emotions, be thankful for the lessons you learned and the awareness you developed as a result.

Be thankful for the chance to recharge and renew when you're asleep.

Finally, think of a happy thought about someone you love and are grateful for in your life.

Manage your fire

Another way of looking at energy in motion within you, is to think of it as a fire; you can decide to fan the flames, or let it burn out. You're the fire officer for your own fires and you have all the equipment you need on hand at any time inside you to decide how much fire you would like. You might not be able to completely control the triggers for the fires –although you will get better at that with practise – but you can observe this energy feeling within you and then decide if you would like to let it burn out if it is unhelpful, or fuel it to flame more if it's helpful.

When my young children have their own little raging emotions from not getting what they want, my wife and I let them burn off steam and calm down before we do anything, and it takes a little time for the energy to change and normal communication to continue. Distractions and thought pattern changes can speed this up, but the stronger the energy charge, the longer it takes to calm. It's the same for all of us at all ages, it's just much more obvious in a two-year-old as they haven't yet learnt to try and disguise how they feel.

As you build your awareness and realise you're in charge, not only will you experience fewer fires but you will know that you can manage them by either fanning them, if they're feelings you want more of, or letting them burn out if they're feelings you want less of. Knowing you have this power over your feelings is an inner strength and will give you the freedom of being able to choose how you want to feel.

We have talked mostly about thoughts triggering chemicals and energy flow, as this is the main way your energy flow is affected, but there are other things that can also affect the electricity and chemicals released in your body. What we put into or bodies, such as food and drugs, and external energy waves such as from the weather, music or electromagnetic activity, will all affect how our electricity and chemicals flow. How you move also affects your energy and chemicals, which is one of the reasons why you feel so good when you exercise.

The power of breath

How you breathe is one of the most underrated capabilities we have that affects how we feel; with every breath, we stimulate millions of cells in our respiratory system and when we change our breathing patterns, we change the messages we send to our brain and the energy flow and chemicals released. Breathing is a hugely important factor in how we feel and if we build more awareness about how we breathe, we can practise breathing techniques to manage our emotion. When you focus on your breathing, you can't be focusing on unhelpful thoughts, and there are physiologically relaxing, scientifically proven benefits from breathing practices. When people talk about having panic attacks, this is usually forgetting to breathe, so in moments of intense emotion, breathe deeply and you'll immediately start calming your ocean of emotion, and releasing physical tension too.

EXERCISE 29
Practise Breathing Awareness

Make yourself comfortable somewhere quiet, either standing or sitting.

Take ten slow, long extra-deep breaths, inhaling and exhaling for five or six seconds each time, breathing in through your nose and out through your mouth. These should be big, diaphragmic breaths where you really feel your chest and upper body expand with each inhale, and deflate with each exhale.

Imagine inhaling new positivity and vitality with each breath in, and imagine you're getting rid of any negativity, unhelpful thoughts and rubbish in your mind, with each deep breath out. Literally, each breath is changing your life.

Pause after a set of ten breaths, then return to breathing in a normal, relaxed state and just be still.

In this stillness, focus your awareness on the energy within you. Be grateful for this energy flow, and for knowing you're in control of this ocean of energy in motion that you are.

Now repeat the deep diaphragmic breaths with two more sets of ten, pausing and focusing again on your energy awareness between each set.

How you breathe is a critical component of your emotional state and there are many breathing techniques you can learn to help you change how you feel. Breathing is a fascinating and essential part of our life, yet learning how we can breathe differently to manage our state gets little attention in conventional education. If you practice yoga or similar activities, you should already be very aware of your breathing and techniques to influence how you feel, and if not, you might want to consider regularly attending a class.

Heart breathing

There is another specific type of breathing that deserves particular attention; a breathing technique that focuses on the heart. Our heart is at our human core and by bringing attention to it as we breathe, we can practice a powerful energy-changing technique known as heart breathing.

The HeartMath Institute, founded by Doc Childre, has carried out extensive research into the heart's intelligence. The heart can be thought of in many ways as our real mind, being the core of our soul and who we are, having started beating before our brain was even created. The heart is our centre of compassion and love, and a feeling of fulfilment is experienced when our mind is aligned with our heart and when we are focused on love or giving. States of 'flow' are experienced when there is coherence between our mind and heart, and the energy and chemicals in that coherent state make us feel very contented.

When your mind is processing negative or stressful thoughts, your brainwaves are out of sync with your heart and this incoherent state causes your energy ocean to flow in a more agitated way, and chemicals are released which affect your feelings. When you have angry or frustrated thoughts, your energy in motion is all out of sync with your heart's energy in motion, and it feels stressful, but when you're actively thinking of gratitude, you're coherent and in flow, and it feels good.

Feeling grateful and loving are states the heart is created for, and are the optimal states of a human life. Learning to breathe through your heart is a technique you can use anytime to feel calm, grateful and to connect with all the love that you are as a human.

EXERCISE 30
Practise Heart Breathing

Find somewhere quiet and sit or stand comfortably, breathing slowly and deeply as in the previous exercise.

Imagine taking these deep slow breaths again, but this time instead of them being through your nose and mouth, think instead of taking breaths into and out of your heart, through your chest rather than your head, as if your heart can breathe. Don't overthink this, just imagine your heart is taking the breaths. If it helps focus, put your hand on your chest where your heart is.

Take ten of these deep breaths, focusing on each inhale going deeply into, and then each exhale releasing out of, your heart. As you do this heart breathing, think of something you are incredibly grateful for in your life. As you think and feel this gratitude, breathe it fully into your heart with each breath in, and then relax and breathe out ready for the next inhale.

After ten, pause for a few moments and then repeat with another ten, and this time think of someone you love. With each breath pour your love from your heart towards this person. It doesn't matter where in the world they are, sitting next to you or in an opposite hemisphere, just send your love outwardly to them.

Pause again after this set of ten deep breaths, and then think of a time in your life when something happened that you thought was a coincidence. Something, somewhere that lead to great joy but which was completely unplanned. Breathe deeply for ten more breaths while doing this, and then pause and reflect on this coincidence. Maybe it was meeting your partner, or a stranger that became a great friend, or maybe someone who gave you advice that changed your life course.

Was it a coincidence or was it life working for you? Be grateful that you are guided and be grateful for the love that created you.

A state of flow

When I was at university, the first book I remember reading was by Mihaly Csikszentmihalyi, titled *Beyond Boredom and Anxiety*. I thought if I could remember that name and regurgitate it in an exam paper it would surely make me appear well-read and authoritative. I'm not sure it worked but I did always remember the core idea and simple message about flow. Your optimal life feeling will be when you are in a state of flow, not thinking anxious thoughts, but also not feeling bored. This is a state we have all likely experienced when participating in a hobby, watching a great film or being lost in an activity we love. When you are in 'flow', your cells are happy and your mind is engaged. This state of flow feels great and effortless and is a reason people can, for example, spend so much time immersed in their hobbies, not bored and not anxious, with just the right (for them) level of stimulation. We can choose to build into our lives as much of this flow state as we can but it's inevitable that we'll get annoyed and frustrated at times, so we need tools to be able to notice these less desirable states early and be able to deal with them before they escalate. Even the top self-improvement and spiritual development 'experts' get frustrated at times; the only difference is that that they're very good at noticing triggers, and catching these thoughts and feelings early.

What are you watching?

In Step 2 we looked at how when we think about something we're mostly creating pictures or a movie in our mind, and the type of movie you make, will determine how you stir the emotional energy within you. Are you stoking and fanning your fires of good feelings like love, joy, excitement when you create images in your mind? Are you making sure any less desirable states like anger and frustration are fizzling out and dissipating? You are in charge of what you fan or extinguish, you are the manager of your energy and you can decide what movies to watch.

EXERCISE 31
Manage the pictures in your mind

Think of something that you feel really annoyed by. It could be anything, but when you think of it, you have frustrated and angry thoughts. Ideally choose a different example than the one you chose for Exercise 26.

What are you seeing and hearing in your mind when you think of this?

From Step 2, you know that when you think of something you are creating pictures in your mind, and you can change the pictures and the way you are looking at them to change the way you feel.

What picture do you see? Is the image large or small, close to you or far away? Is the image in colour or black and white? Moving or still? Loud or quiet?

Become more aware of the detail in your pictures and know that you can manage these images, and produce different ones if the current ones aren't working for you.

Draw a border around this picture which is making you annoyed, like you did in Exercise 21.

When it has its border, shrink it right down, drain the colour, move it far away and turn the sound down. This is often called 'changing the sub-modalities'.

Adjusting these aspects of your imagining, allows you to disempower the images that are annoying you, which subsequently causes different electric and chemical charges within you.

You are the manager and producer of what you choose to watch and how you choose to feel.

Try the exercise again but now also replace old unhelpful pictures with more helpful and fun pictures.

Make better pictures and movies and you'll feel better. It's as simple as that. You are the producer and director of your own mind art and mind movies so you can decide to watch anything you choose. Much of the processing is happening in our unconscious mind so it's critical that we are managing and programming our mind using the tools we suggested in Step 2.

The impact of fear

Think of something that makes you fearful. Fear is usually thought of in a negative way but as we said earlier, fear can be incredibly useful in life and is part of our survival nature, helping raise awareness of, or encouraging us to remove ourselves from, dangerous and harmful situations. When we think fearful thoughts, our body increases its heartbeat and respiration rate in order to provide the energy and oxygen that will be needed to fuel a rapid response to perceived danger. Blood flow to the surface areas of the body is reduced and the flow to the muscles, brain, legs and arms is increased. Your face might become pale, or you may alternate between pale and flushed as blood rushes to your head. The body's blood-clotting ability also increases in order to prevent excess blood loss in the event of injury. The body prepares itself to be more aware and alert during times of danger with the dilation of the pupils, which allows more light into the eyes and your muscles become tense and primed for action which can result in trembling or shaking. All that natural physiological change just from some fearful thoughts.

We should be grateful for the feelings we have that alert us, but fearful thoughts can also sometimes be debilitating, irrational and stop us from doing stuff we really want to do. Fear is essentially imagining a bad outcome of something that hasn't happened yet. Phobias are excessive and irrational thoughts. We can change how we think to change how we feel and get rid of these irrational fears by creating more helpful pictures in our minds. The most common excessive fears include flying, spiders, rats, public speaking and heights.

"You are born with only two fears: fear of falling and fear of loud noise. All the rest is learned. And it's a lot of work!"– Richard Bandler

Irrational fear

Rational fear we know is helpful. For example, you wouldn't want to get too close to an edge with a huge drop, and staying away from rats is generally a good idea so as not to catch disease, but phobias can hold us back. With phobias, the mind has created a movie which causes the energy flow and physiological responses in a particularly debilitating way, but if we just change the movies we're playing to ourselves, we'll change how we feel and how we react. If you get a chance to attend some of Richard Bandler's excellent Neuro Linguistic Programming seminars, you will see first-hand how people with extreme phobias of snakes, spiders and public speaking change the movies they play in their minds and immediately change their feelings about what they previously feared.

Estimates suggest as many as 25% of adults are scared of flying. When someone is scared of flying, what movie do you think they're making when they take a flight? Are they thinking how confined they are? Imagining the plane crashing, falling out of the sky and all the passengers dying? Whatever the specifics, they're likely making a movie in their mind of all the terrible things they imagine could go wrong. How is that going to make their energy flow? With phobias, it's just the thought of flying that causes the image, not actually getting on a plane, and those who suffer with phobias are very good at making vivid movies about something that hasn't happed yet. They are making it up, or imagining the worst and they are actually very good movie-makers.

What if they made an equally vivid movie but this time focusing on a much better outcome? Perhaps picturing themselves relaxing, having some well-deserved 'me time' and being waited on as they choose what to do. A time to be calm, read, watch a documentary, a time to plan and to think about the excitement ahead. What energy reaction is that kind of movie going to create?

EXERCISE 32
Dealing with Irrational Fear

If you are 'doing' excessive fearful thinking to the level it is debilitating, try this simple process of breathing and more helpful movie making.

Start with breathing; take deeper breaths to relax from tension and change your energy flow. You can change the depth and pace of your breaths as we have already done in previous exercises. Enjoy the feeling of release when you exhale after a long deep inhale.

When you are experiencing fear, you're thinking fearful thoughts as you play a movie in your mind that reinforces these thoughts and which causes your energy to move in a particular way.

Now imagine something specific that you're really fearful of. It could be flying, seeing spiders or public speaking. It doesn't matter.

Notice the movie this triggers, and then step out of the movie and imagine you're watching it on a large cinema screen. See yourself sitting, relaxed in your cinema armchair. You're watching the film, rather than being in it.

Imagine you have a remote-control device in your hand to manage how the movie plays.

As you are watching it play, when you are ready, press the pause button. Take a few deep breaths and then fast forward to the end. It is a boring and unhelpful film you've played many times so let's get to the end. Pause when you arrive at the end frame.

Now press fast rewind and watch the film rewind back. Notice how it's scrambled and how all the colour and sound is draining from it. When it reaches the beginning, it has virtually faded away and it culminates in a final little puff of smoke and disappears into the distance.

You have erased the film, and are now able to produce a much more helpful one.

Play a new film, one you that create, where you're in control. Visualise yourself calmly doing what you previously feared. It feels so much better. At end of your new film, pause and celebrate.

You now know how to erase crap films and make new ones. It's all in your imagination! Your mind is in your control, so make great films. Why watch rubbish ones?

You can repeat this process as often as you like. The key point is to step out of the film and watch yourself in it, pressing the fast forward and then the rewind scramble until it becomes drained and disappears in a puff of smoke.

Scared of public speaking?

In the US, fear of public speaking is reported as the most common excessive fear, with estimates claiming related anxiety affects as many as 75% of adults. If someone says they are scared of public speaking, what's actually happening is that they're making rubbish films about imagining themselves in front of an audience. Their movies will usually include freezing or forgetting what to say, feeling humiliated and just wanting the ground to swallow them up as the audience laughs at their embarrassment. With that kind of movie playing, how do you think someone is going to feel? Their energy is going to flow in an unhelpful way, driven by these thoughts, and the physiological responses will follow.

Imagine if, however, their movie was about walking in front of the audience confidently, smiling, totally in control, and being really liked, everyone laughing at their jokes and being completely engaging? I'm sure you are getting the picture – no pun intended. Whether it's a fear of flying, public speaking, heights, spiders or snakes, the brain process is the same, and we can all take charge of the processes and 'do' them differently. When we decide to improve our thinking processes, the energy will flow differently and the body will react in ways that are designed to help us.

Physiological responses

At some point, you will have felt your stomach churn or your heart palpate from anxious thoughts. These physiological responses, such as sweaty palms or a racing heartbeat, are regulated by your nervous system. The most basic of these physiological changes are associated with the upper chest area, and likely correspond to changes in breathing and heartrate, but there are lots of changes in our bodies as a result of our thoughts. The autonomic nervous system controls involuntary body responses, such as blood flow and digestion whereas the sympathetic nervous system is charged with controlling the body's 'fight or flight' reactions.

When you are facing a threat, these responses automatically prepare your body to either flee from danger or face the threat. Brain scans have shown that a tiny almond-shaped structure in the brain, the amygdala, plays an important role in stirring emotion from fearful thoughts, in particular.

Brain-imaging has been used to show that when people are shown threatening images, the amygdala becomes activated. A network of neural pathways connects the amygdala to the other parts of the brain, allowing us to reflect on our feelings and to think before acting. In times of perceived crisis, however, those pathways are bypassed and impulse overrides reason with a kind of emotional hijacking in which the amygdala takes over the brain. It's therefore wise to be mindful of your emotional state if conversations get heated.

Angry thoughts flood the brain with catecholamines, which are hormones that prime the body for action and stimulate the nervous system, putting it on a general state of alert. Someone who is already in a bad mood will remain edgy and more easily aroused to anger than someone who is not, so it's smart to be tuned into your energy in motion, your electricity and chemicals, and take charge of dissipating any unhelpful feelings to bring your ocean of emotion back to a calmer state. There is a chain of rapidly occurring reactions inside the body when someone is 'doing' angry thoughts, helping to mobilise the body's resources to deal with threatening circumstances. This results in an increase in heartrate, blood pressure, and breathing rate. After the threat is gone, it can take between 20 to 60 minutes for the body to return to its pre-arousal levels.

"Make a speech when you are angry and it will be the best speech you will ever regret." –Anon

EXERCISE 33
Adopt the Two-minute Rule

You understand it is inevitable that many things in life will simply not go your way.

However, agree from this moment, that you are only ever going to allow yourself to feel bad for two minutes at any time. Rather than unrealistically saying "I'm never going to feel crap," just put a limit on it and know you are in control.

Anytime you become aware you are doing angry thoughts, focus on the feelings this thinking is causing. You now understand what is happening and the storm of energy in motion that will be starting to build. Acknowledge it, be grateful for its intention even if it's not necessary, and then let it fizzle out by focusing on your breathing and controlling the process.

You can change how you feel with techniques like breathing differently, moving, or changing focus so you are in the control seat. You decide. And two minutes is more than enough time to allow yourself to feel crap, don't you think?

You already own the best medicine

According to the American Medical Association, stress contributes to around 75% of all cases of illnesses in the United States. Your body physically changes due to the chemicals released by any stressful thoughts. For example, your blood pressure goes up when you do angry thoughts or your heart rate rises when you do fearful thoughts. Taking charge of your emotions is one of the best medicines, has no negative side effects, is free and doesn't require an appointment with a doctor.

In Step 2, we looked at how our brain processes information through our senses, and it is no coincidence our sensory organs are near our brain. Your brain processes all the information it receives based on your previous experiences, and the values and beliefs you have programmed, and it thinks thoughts. The thinking processes release chemicals which cause reactions. Although there are many recipes of chemicals and these are changing all the time in our dynamic biochemistry, the actual biological function of all these chemicals is complex and multifaceted, affecting numerous physiological processes. There is much research and material you can read about biochemistry, but for the purposes of the SYSO System and changing your life, you don't need to know everything, just that there are some key chemicals it's useful to have a basic understanding of, and most importantly know what you can do to *manage your biochemistry for the feelings you want.*

Dopamine is the chemical responsible for reward-driven behavior and pleasure-seeking. In simple terms, if you want to get a hit of feel-good dopamine, set a goal and achieve it. Dopamine brings feelings of pleasure based on a certain action, and every time a response to something results in a reward, the pathways and associations between brain cells become stronger by increasing the intensity at which they respond to particular stimuli. In an evolutionary sense, we're rewarded for beneficial behaviours and motivated to repeat them. Many addictive drugs for example, such as cocaine and methamphetamine, act directly on the dopamine system, but you don't need drugs. You can increase your levels of dopamine naturally by flooding your brain through setting goals and achieving them.

Another chemical, **serotonin**, is involved in mood and perception. Low serotonin levels are believed to lead to depressive thoughts and feelings, anger management issues and difficulty sleeping, although it plays many different roles in our bodies. It's like the body's natural tranquiliser, as it relaxes us, regulates body temperature and appetite, sets our internal clock for sleep, and makes us feel peaceful and contented. People with low levels of serotonin tend to act rashly and aggressively and have what has too commonly been referred to as low mood. If you want to increase your serotonin, do things that reinforce a sense of purpose, meaning and accomplishment. Popular antidepressants tend to focus on serotonin and drugs called serotonin-specific reuptake inhibitors are widely prescribed to treat a range of low serotonin disorders, but there's a big question as to whether these 'antidepressants' are dished out too frequently. In the UK, for example, around 7 million people are taking antidepressants. However, our bodies can create serotonin and other feel good chemicals without drugs and without the side effects and the cost of these medications.

"We need to provide no-drug routes back to happiness." – Rachel Kelly

Oxytocin is another feel-good chemical messenger and is directly linked to human connection and bonding. New parents, particularly mothers, get a big hit of oxytocin when their child is born. Also called the 'love hormone', oxytocin is believed to make people feel close and contented, and their hearts calm. Some researchers suggest this may explain why happily coupled people usually live longer than single people.

Endorphins, the next group of chemicals, are associated with pleasure feelings and pain relief and the name endorphin actually translates to 'self-produced morphine'. Endorphins are produced during strenuous physical exertion, such as running, dancing and having orgasms, and in many ways, they are a natural painkiller and soother.

Endocannabinoids are increasingly called the 'bliss molecules' and it may be that they are more specifically responsible for what we call runners high. **Gamma-Aminobutyric acid (GABA)** is a molecule that slows down the firing of neurons and creates a sense of calmness. You can produce this naturally by practicing yoga or meditation, for example.

Adrenaline is like an energy molecule and plays a large role in our human fight or flight mechanism; its release is exhilarating and creates a surge in energy. It causes an increase in heartrate and blood pressure, and works by constricting less important blood vessels to increase blood flow to larger muscles. An 'adrenaline rush' comes in times of distress or facing fearful situations, but it can be triggered on demand by doing, or imagining, things that scare you or feel dangerous.

These are just some of the more commonly referred-to neurochemicals, and not only are there many, many more, they'll be released in different strengths and different blends with other chemicals. The important point is that these chemicals affect how you feel and you can create and manage them by controlling your thinking. Make chemicals and energy flows that make you feel good and you won't need any chemicals in the form of toxic medicines, or unhealthy foods, which aim to give you these types of chemicals artificially.

Once you're aware of what's happening with your neurochemicals and how these are influenced by thoughts, you can catch yourself earlier and better manage the chemical responses and feelings you have. What and how we think causes so much change in our body, and this has a big knock-on effect. You can also use this to your advantage by being proactive about managing your thinking so you can consciously prime your body – using breathing and movement – to be better prepared to perform in any situation.

"Emotions are what makes us human, make us real. The word 'emotion' stands for energy in motion. Be truthful about your emotions, and use your mind and emotions in your favour, not against yourself." – Robert Kiyosaki

By now you should be starting to see that emotion and chemical changes in your body are human resources available to help you, but that you need to take charge and control these if you want them to work for you. Emotion is electrical and biochemical. It's all about your body and it could be that your thoughts and feelings occur not just in the brain as has been traditionally thought, but in virtually every system and cell of your body, which are all inextricably linked in your nervous system. Thoughts are translated into chemical expressions, or 'codes', by our bodies, and are then communicated through our various intimately connected body systems. It's therefore no surprise that there's increasing emphasis on the interaction of mind and body in health studies and medicine.

Movement and music

One of the most important things we can do to release chemicals in our bodies, to change how the energy travels and how we feel, is to move. Movement and exercise cause chemicals to be released and also wakes up your cells. You're likely aware of feeling good when you have exercised. Apart from stimulating your cells, when you exercise you release endorphins, dopamine and serotonin which creates a great cocktail of feel-good chemicals. Moving your body is vitally important in how you feel and if you're experiencing any unhelpful emotions, exercise is always a good place to start.

Emotion and chemicals are also stimulated through each of your senses. For example, we all know music has the potential to change how we feel and in Step 1 we learnt that music is made up of pressure waves and that different waves can makes us feel differently. Music has often been called the 'sound of our emotions' and this may be an accurate representation. The waves affect our energy in motion and the thoughts we have when we process lyrics, together with patterns of vibrations, release chemicals.

Additionally, what we see, such as art and nature, and what we taste, can change our biochemistry and energy flows. Stimulation through touch, massage and of course sex, also affects energy and chemicals in various ways. When someone says the sex wasn't electric or the chemistry wasn't right, there is some scientific truth in this.

Altogether, we have plenty of tools to change how we feel at any time and to take charge of our emotional responses. Whether it's how we think, how we move, listening to music, eating, drinking, tactile experiences, looking at nature or art, smelling perfume or flowers, all these stimulations cause electric and chemical reactions.

Moreover, research is increasingly showing that emotion affects our immunity. By being in charge of our energy flow we can increase our resilience to disease, and stay healthier for longer. Feel good and live longer! Pretty compelling reasons to take charge of your natural chemicals, don't you think?!

Choose how you want to feel

Emotional energy is different at different times and it ebbs and flows, but the principle remains the same. Our chemistry changes and our senses change but we can still decide at any time how we want to feel and having that power within yourself is about the most liberating thing you can feel. Never again buy into excuses like 'my emotions got the better of me'. Choose how you want to feel and know you are running your emotions, not the other way around. Nothing outside you can annoy you – 'being annoyed' is something you do to yourself. People can't insult you; you allow yourself to be insulted.

We now know that instead of thinking of different specific emotions existing within us, it's much more helpful to think of emotion as the energy within us which moves primarily in relation to our thoughts and our physiology. We are in control, not at the mercy of our emotion and we don't have to label differences in this energy movement. Instead, start examining the type of thoughts we have. We've discussed that emotion flowing through your body is just electricity and chemicals, and you can specifically condition yourself to be in charge of this emotional energy to work for you. You're still going to experience crap in your life which will make you feel bad and push your energy in motion in unhelpful ways; the key is that when you're in charge, you can let it burn out quickly and not engulf you. You can catch your unhelpful processes much quicker and deal with them earlier before the fire gets out of hand. Being aware gives you the power to decide on how you will feel and to take control of your emotions before your emotions take control of you.

EXERCISE 34
Dealing with Disappointment

Many things in your life will not go the way you had hoped or planned. Guaranteed! Some of the disappointments will be bigger than others, but you can use the following simple 4-step technique to manage how you deal with anything that comes your way. Disappointments will happen, and most of it will be out of your control, but you can control how you respond by changing how you think to change how you feel.

Step 1: Whenever something doesn't go your way, say to yourself, as we covered in Exercise 27: "It could be worse." We know it always could be. This immediately helps you keep a healthy perspective on what has happened, and is a form of gratitude as you are being grateful whatever happened isn't worse.

Step 2: We know it could always be worse, but now expand that thought outwards and see yourself floating above your life, looking at it from above from start to finish. Has crap happened in the past? Did life go on without much drama? Did you learn from it? As you look down on all the time of your life you can see this moment of disappointment is nothing more than a redirection you hadn't expected. It will soon pass, as everything passes.

Step 3: Ask yourself what are you learning from this? You will be learning something, and by focusing on the lessons, you detract from focusing on the disappointment.

Step 4: Move your body to make your energy flow differently and to change the chemical mix inside you. Jump up and down, punch the air, wave your arms, clap, breathe deeply or whatever movement works for you. If you are in a public place and don't feel comfortable leaping around, just clench your fist discreetly. There are many ways you can change your body, to change the energy flow and to wake up your cells, letting your mind know you are in charge.

If you practise these 4 steps repeatedly, this simple process will become habitual. You will just run this unconsciously any time crap happens. Realising it could be worse, keeping perspective, acknowledging the learning, and making a physiological change, are the 4 steps to dealing with anything that doesn't go your way.

Start your day with a gratitude smile

How you start your day is very important in managing your emotional state and it is invaluable to develop a positive habitual morning routine. Win the morning, win the day, as the saying goes. It's essential to set your day up intentionally, giving your unconscious mind clear directions and to awaken the cells in your body. Start your day with gratitude and movement and set your focus for the day and life ahead. Smile, starting each morning appreciating the amazingness that is life, and condition yourself to sail through your day feeling great and thankful whatever happens. If you do that, your life will be a beautiful journey and a gift to those around you.

When you truly take charge of your emotions, you can live in a great emotional state, experiencing a beautiful flow of energy in motion within you. You can always choose to feel good and it really boils down to what you focus on, what meaning you are giving things and what your body is doing. Give your unconscious mind an express route to feeling great, and a slow and undesirable route to feeling crap. Emotion is your feeling of being alive, and now you know you can choose how to feel, why not choose to always feel awesome and grateful no matter what happens?

EXERCISE 35
Keep Perspective

Sit down, make yourself comfortable and relax. Take some deep breaths.

As you sit, point to where your future is and point to where your past was. Just instinctively, where you see the future and where you see the past.

For most people, the past will be behind and the future ahead, although it doesn't matter, just go with whatever feels right for you.

Now draw an imaginary line from the past to the future which, we will call your journey line.

As you sit in the current moment, imagine you are sitting in a clear, lightweight, super-safe bubble that moves where you want it to. You have some simple controls in front of you that move the bubble up and down, and forward and back, as fast or slow as you choose.

At any time, by pulling the joystick, you can float up above your life, higher and higher, and look down on the path of your journey line from birth to where you are now. The past has passed and you can be grateful for getting this far, and for the invaluable lessons you have gained in preparation for the future. As you rise up you can see all you have gone through, and so many times that seemed frustrating or disappointing. All the times you were running processes in your mind of anger, all passed and all likely now seem so inconsequential.

Now look to the future, and see a brightness ahead, and feel grateful you get to create the future you want.

With your new 'perspective bubble', you can float above your life any time and see things in a more helpful perspective. You can fly back over your journey line and hover above any times or incidents that you keep remembering as 'bad', and which cause you to think painful thoughts.

Lower yourself in your bubble to each of the 'bad' moments you remember and then reach out and remove a storage stick that has all the bad memories on it. Now replace each with a new gleaming memory stick loaded with better memories and gratitude for what each experience gave you.

At any time, you can travel back and forth along and above your journey line and you can control the memories stored in your mind by replacing them with more helpful versions and being grateful for the learnings.

You can also visualise the future you want and which you are going to create.

Enjoy your travels, reframing the past, imagining the future and always keeping perspective.

In summary, you can't control what goes on outside of you, but you can always control your responses and your thinking, which controls how your energy flows. In Western culture, we have evolved with a brain-centric approach to living but now it's time for a much more heart-centric approach, leading with our hearts not our egos.

Aristotle believed: "*Happiness is the meaning and the purpose of life, the whole aim and end of human existence.*" Maybe he was partly right; happiness for everyone is a great goal, but the main vehicle is love. Love is energy, perhaps in its purest life form, and when you focus on being and giving love, the feeling you get is the energy flow that is most aligned with the ultimate life force flow for you and the universe. When you give love, you first must feel it inside you. Love is a core human need as you will see in Step 4 and you are entirely in charge of the love you give, and therefore what you feel.

"Your task is not to seek for love, but merely to seek and find all the barriers within yourself that you have built against it." – Rumi

STEP 4
Understand Your Needs

"All human actions are an attempt to meet needs" – Marshall Rosenberg

We know from Step 1 that there are over 7 billion individual versions of humans alive on Planet Earth today. Each life is a distinct work of art, different but equal, and we think and feel in our own nuanced ways. There are 7 billion versions of reality being experienced right now as a blend of chemicals and life force energy in each person's body. These forces within cause us to feel how we feel, but we have tools at our disposal to take charge of these forces and manage our thinking and emotion for the life we want. If we don't take charge, we'll simply be passengers reacting to thoughts and feelings as they arise from programming we didn't design.

Our core human needs

We also, as part of our unique core human operating system, have inbuilt needs or drivers which motivate and guide us to do what we do. These drivers are embedded within us, and are part of what it is to be human. They are our core human needs and if we cleared out all the programming installed since birth, we would still have these inbuilt human drivers. We all share these same needs, and we're all trying to meet these needs through our behaviour. What I buy, the way I act, the way I live is all driven by trying to meet my core human needs. I am driven to try and meet all these needs but the order in which I prioritise them, and the way in which I try to meet them, will determine my experience of, and degree of fulfilment in, my life. Most people aren't aware of these core needs driving their life as most of the processing is happening unconsciously, but bringing awareness of these needs and how they shape what you do into your consciousness is one of the most important things you can do to change your life.

"Nature provides enough to satisfy human needs." – Seneca

As humans, we are above all else programmed to try and stay alive. This survival instinct is a fundamental basic driver which we, and all living creatures, share and without which we would be extinct. It doesn't matter if a child is born in China, Namibia, Peru or New Zealand, or as part of a remote tribal group deep in the Amazon rainforest; every single human being has an inbuilt, pre-programmed, human drive to try and stay alive. It doesn't mean we will survive, it just means we are driven to try to, and it's our most basic primal evolutionary force. We all need oxygen, food and water or we will die and we need to be protected from the elements with some form of shelter and security. These needs for survival are basic and obvious to most of us, although usually taken for granted in developed countries.

Once these needs are met and we have food and feel safe, there are other inbuilt needs, or core operational programming, which are part of what makes us human and which we are always striving to meet. By being aware of and understanding all of these human drivers, we can better appreciate why we and others do the things we do. Through personal development work, we can become more aware of ways to meet these needs that are helpful for the life we want rather than in unhelpful ways that block our path to feeling truly fulfilled. We can also learn the importance of prioritising different human needs to cause different outcomes in our experience of life.

Psychologists and academics have long understood there are basic human drivers in all of us, and there have been many theories suggested to describe and explain what these are. Perhaps the most well-known is Abraham Maslow's theory of human needs developed back in the 1940s. It was Maslow who proposed that needs are hierarchical in that each need has to be met before moving to the next.

Maslow believed that people move through five stages, or levels, in pursuit of what they desire in life. Physiological needs – such as shelter, food, rest, come first – and then safety, belongingness/love, self-esteem and, finally, self-actualisation. These different stages are usually taught by showing a pyramid shape with self-actualisation sitting at the top. Only once we have met our survival needs will humans seek out the next levels. If you are starving, for example, you're not likely to be very concerned about whether your relationships are a joy, or whether you feel fulfilled. You will strive to meet your basic survival need of food first so you stay alive and then you'll start being interested in the other areas of your life and feeling safe and connected. 'Foodfilled' always comes first!

Later in his career, Maslow added that he believed we only find self-actualisation or fulfilment in giving ourselves to some higher outside goal, in altruism and spirituality. He equated this with the desire to reach what he later called the transcendence stage at the very top of his revised pyramid, and this idea forms the basis of most personal development theory today.

"Transcendence refers to the very highest and most inclusive or holistic levels of human consciousness, behaving and relating, as ends rather than means, to oneself, to significant others, to human beings in general, to other species, to nature, and to the cosmos." – Abraham Maslow

Maslow's work provided the basis for lots of other theories on embedded human needs, although most are really just variations of his ideas. Some have suggested needs such as safety, security, love, self-esteem, fulfilment and freedom are sought simultaneously all the time, whereas others believe in the more hierarchical way of looking at behaviour drivers. Some suggest even simpler classifications. The SYSO System is very practical and so it is not necessary to know all the different theories, but it can be helpful to understand just some of the more prominent ones.

A very simple theory was put forward by Clayton Alderfer, who suggested an adaption to Maslow's hierarchy, where he claims people simply seek three things in life: Existence, Relatedness and Growth. David McClelland kept it simple too, also claiming that there are only three core needs that are fundamental drivers of what we do; the need for achievement, the need for a sense of belonging, and the need to feel in control.

Paul Lawrence and Nitin Nohira suggest there are four key drives that determine how we behave. The first is to acquire what we need for survival, conception and looking after our offspring. Second, to defend ourselves and our family from threats. Third, to bond with others and form long-term, mutually caring and trusting relationships, and finally, to comprehend to learn, create, innovate and make sense of the world and our place in it. This really just boils down to survival, building relationships and growth.

Susan Fiske proposes five core drivers: belonging, understanding, controlling, enhancing self and trusting. Belonging, she suggests, is the fundamental core motive which drives all of us and that we are at our best when tightly connected into social networks, but we suffer the most when we are lonely and disconnected. The American psychiatrist William Glasser, again like Fiske, believed the most important need is for love and belonging but in his view, we are all driven by our genes to also satisfy the needs of survival, power, freedom and fun.

If we go back 150 years or so, even Charles Darwin was thinking and writing about human drivers, claiming that the most important distinction between us as humans and what he called the 'lower species' is our conscience as a basic evolutionary driving force. Darwin believed humans have endured as a species because we learned to work in groups and rely on problem-solving skills, rather than just physical force. That sense of belongingness or togetherness is again seen as central to our human drive.

Sigmund Freud proposed that there are only two basic drives that serve to motivate all our thoughts, emotions and behaviour. Simply reduced to sex and aggression, also called Eros and Thanatos, or life and death. He also believed we develop from birth our id, our ego and then our superego and that these states of ourselves go a long way to explaining why we behave the way we do at a basic level. Sex as a primary driving force for humans was a key theme for Freud, and is a basic force in all animals to ensure the survival of a species.

"Understanding human needs is half the job of meeting them." – Adlai Stevenson

From theory to action

Amongst all the theories that touch on human needs – and only a small number are mentioned here to give you a flavour – there are some great intellectual writings, but the question to ask is: What can we actually take from these theories to then make a difference in our lives? Understanding may be 'half the job', but only action will change your life in the direction you want. Analysing can sometimes become 'anal-ising'. We need to be action-ising not anal-ising if we are to make effective life changes. This book is about what we can actually *do*, what action we can take to make our lives magnificent.

In terms of all the theories, there are certainly some common themes and ways of classifying our human needs. The SYSO System suggests that the easiest way to think about these embedded needs is that there are really three types or groups of needs with their nuances and blends being different for each of us. Firstly, we have the need to survive, then we have the needs of our personality and finally the needs of our spirit. So, we have Survival, Personality and Spiritual needs. To feel really fulfilled in life, you need to meet all three of these needs. When we go deeper into the detail of what each of these needs groups include, it's clear that in different situations and different phases of our life we naturally value different aspects of these needs groups for different reasons. However, in simple terms, presuming you have satisfied your survival needs, it's in meeting your personality and spiritual needs in healthy ways that you will unlock feelings of fulfilment and joy in your life.

It is in these areas of personality and spiritual human needs that I believe the work of Tony Robbins is probably the most useful and practical. Maslow's ideas were hugely valuable and Robbins evolved these and other theories in presenting his overview of the underlying motivating forces driving our decisions in life. Every day we make choices and take actions based on what we think and Robbins' work invites us to examine the six needs we constantly work to satisfy at a mostly unconscious level, and how through awareness and regular conditioning, we can take charge of these forces in a practical way, to work in creating the life we want.

If you have ever attended one of Robbins' events, you will almost certainly have heard the importance of understanding what he describes as these universal human needs and how you can change how you prioritise and meet these needs to effect radical change in your life. Robbins is a phenomenal expression of human life force and he has committed himself relentlessly over 40 years to help people make the most of their lives. So much of his work is to be admired for his ability to simplify the seemingly complex, but also for its practical application and inspirational delivery, and he always projects his messages in a fun and humble way, with incredible high energy.

Six core needs

In Robbins' theory, we are always trying to meet six core needs as part of our human make up. These needs influence our deepest motivations and determine how we go about prioritising our decisions and actions. We journey through stages of life where our focus and our priorities may be different, but we all have these six needs we are always trying to meet through our behaviour. The key is *how* we are trying to meet these needs – whether helpfully or unhelpfully – and how we are prioritising them. How we value these six needs and in what order determines the direction of our life.

> *"Whatever emotion you're after, whatever vehicle you pursue—building a business, getting married, raising a family, traveling the world—whatever you think your nirvana is, there are six basic, universal needs that make us tick and drive all human behaviour."* – *Tony Robbins*

So, let's get familiar with these universal six inbuilt human needs, and we can then start building the neural networks of understanding and the action-activating thoughts to change our behaviour. Understanding and acting in healthy ways to meet these six needs and the priority in which you meet them, will change your life

1. The Need for Certainty

We all have embedded within us the need to feel stable, safe and secure in our world. This is a basic survival need – we need to know the sun will rise and that there is oxygen in the air to breathe. We need to feel in control, know we have basic comfort, can avoid pain and to also believe there will be some enjoyment.

Our need for certainty affects how much risk we are willing to take in all areas of our life and the more of a priority and the more extreme we make this, the more we need to feel in control of everything. In some parts of our life, this need for certainty can be very helpful but in others it is unhelpful.

The world and other people's lives are constantly changing, and so sometimes our need for certainty can cause us to build a wall of controls around our life, which can lead to us wanting to stay in our comfort zone and resist changes. However, we simply can't be in control of everything, and it's important that we don't try to control that which we can't possibly control, as this will lead to immense frustration. Imagine, for example, if I wanted to control the weather or the rotation of the earth; it would be an impossible task and I would drive myself crazy if I made that level of control important to me. This is an extreme example but there is so much in our lives that we can't control or be certain about, especially other people's behaviour. If we are behaving as a 'control freak' in interpersonal relationships and if we need that level of certainty, this will likely cause problems.

If I want a rich and fulfilling life, it will involve trying new experiences, and if I am rigid and extreme in my need for certainty, I will often not want to risk trying things that are new. If certainty is your lead human need, life is going to often feel stressful and frustrating as there will always be a lot that is uncertain.

We can't control so much in the world, but we can however always control how we respond and this certainty of being able to control our response is how to meet our need for certainty in an empowering and positive way. Creating a sense of centeredness, stability and self-belief within us is a positive and healthy way to meet this need. Absolute certainty from within gives the ultimate sense of security in life. The world changes and when we let go of trying to control external factors and trust in the process of life, we understand that one of the main certainties of life is change.

2. The Need for Variety (or Uncertainty!)

Just as we each need to experience a sense of certainty in the world, it would be pretty boring if we knew everything that was going to happen. 'Variety is the spice of life' as the saying goes, and we all need to feel uncertainty so we can grow as humans. When we step outside our comfort zone, we have an opportunity to grow and this interrupts patterns of predictability and stagnation, allowing us to expand ourselves and experience more of who we are and who we can be. When we let go of 'needing to know', we enter a realm of possibility that isn't bound by past experience and memories. 'Knowing that we don't know' can be incredibly liberating, and when we ask bigger questions about life, there is much we can never know in this lifetime.

Our efforts to satisfy the need for variety can, however, be taken to extremes if our primary driver is constant change, and we may find ourselves moving homes, changing relationships and searching for new jobs regularly. This constant change can lead to less stability and make it difficult to feel fulfilled. Satisfying the need for variety by constantly changing our external surroundings can prevent us from fully engaging with life right where we are, but learning and growing and trying new experiences builds us as humans, enabling us to become more and feel fulfilled by meeting this need in healthy ways.

3. The Need for Significance

We all want to be seen, validated and to feel special for who we are and what we do. The question is how much of a priority in your life is it for you to feel significant and how does this affect your behaviour and how you feel? We don't exist in isolation in life (more on this in Step 6) but are part of a greater whole, and to be an effective part of that whole, we need to know that we're important. Satisfying our need for significance is part of creating our sense of identity and who we are in the world, but the challenge with fulfilling this need is when we become dependent on validation from others in order to feel good about ourselves.

We all need to feel important, and you can meet this need by making and showing others how much money you have, how famous you are, by collecting academic qualifications, by buying expensive watches, designer labels, getting tattoos or by building a huge following on social media. Getting significance in this way however, involves comparing ourselves to others, and there will always be someone doing better. The pressure to show off can be stressful and exhausting. We're encouraged to be more significance-driven by social media where we can project and compare 24/7. 'Look at me' culture, celebrity focus and reality TV all play to our need to feel significant.

Feeling significant by external means is never going to make you feel fulfilled as this is superficial and you'll be at the mercy of what others think of you. When you stop comparing yourself to others and seeking their approval, instead focusing on getting validation from yourself, your need for significance in unhealthy ways will dissipate.

When we find significance within, we don't need approval from others. An example of significance being fulfilled in a positive way is when we do something that is helpful for others. We feel significant and worthy when we are of service to others. If you feel you have low self-worth, go and do something for someone else. You will have been of worth to them which will immediately answer your feeling of low self-worth. Giving is a key to a healthy feeling of significance in life and it doesn't have to be material giving. We can give kindness, our time, our listening and our advice as well as our physical help.

When you lower the priority of needing significance from external factors in your life and instead look to feel significant from within, you'll be on a much more powerful and fulfilling path. Connecting more to the spiritual dimension of who you are and impressing yourself with your achievements, rather than wanting to impress others, are healthy ways to meet this need.

Spending a lot of money can make you feel significant, and so can spending very little. Some people constantly brag about their bargains, or they feel special because they have the most eco-friendly home possible. Some very wealthy people gain significance by hiding their wealth and others by showboating and buying flash cars. This form of significance will ultimately feel hollow. Unfortunately, social media and society are driving us to meet our need for significance in unhealthy ways and it can a be a very lucrative need for businesses to tap into. People will often pay a large premium to be seen in the 'coolest' place or to stand out from the crowd with ostentatious displays of luxury, paying over the odds for items they don't need in a practical sense but which make them feel important or special. It isn't that they require the latest handbag, the biggest mansion, the most expensive jewellery, it's usually what they believe having these things will say about them and what others will think.

"Scarcity of self-value cannot be remedied by money, recognition, affection, attention or influence." – Gary Zukav

Thorstein Veblen coined the term conspicuous consumption back in 1899, in his book *The Theory of the Leisure Class*, and significance as a big human driver has been within us since humans existed. I have always been interested in why people wear brand logos so much, and having worked in brand and product marketing at Nike and Adidas for 12 years, I've done my part in fuelling that demand. Of course, brands can be differentiated in terms of design, quality and functionality, but even where products are virtually identical and from the same factories but just labelled differently, the branding or logos can completely change the demand. People wear them not just for the functionality or design, they're often choosing to wear the logos to meet their need to feel significant. We wear logos in the expectation that other people will think about us in a particular way, depending on the brand we are wearing. At the heart of our label craving often lies insecurity about who we are and we seek validation from others as we want them to know we are 'cool' or associated with what we think the particular logo stands for.

At SYSO, we created the **EGO HERE®** brand as a tongue in cheek way to encourage a conversation about how much of our lives are led by our EGO and craving to feel significant. Whether it's wearing logos, flash watches, look-at-me fashion pieces or personal number plates, the motivation is usually to feed our EGO and seek validation (which is really love) from outside ourselves.

The **EGO HERE®** brand advocates leading with our hearts, not our EGO, as a key to living a fulfilled life, and we encourage everyone to question how much of their lives are spent looking for approval from others? A share of profits from the sale of **EGO HERE®** products go to the SYSO Foundation which provides personal development resources to young people to help them avoid becoming messed up older people. You can join the conversation and help change lives by shopping for **EGO HERE®** products at www.syso.life or www.youdontneedtherapy.com.

4. The Need for Love and Connection

We all have a need to love and be loved by others and to feel connected. This is at the core of our human nature. We're in the womb for around nine months and we're dependent on love as a baby to survive and grow. Love created us and we need other's love to feel alive, so it should be no surprise that love and connection with others is central to our experience of fulfilment in life.

"Love is the oxygen of life; it's what we all want and need most. When we love completely we feel alive, but when we lose love, the pain is so great that most people settle on connection, the crumbs of love." – *Tony Robbins*

We can meet this need for love, like all needs, in positive or negative ways. We can get that sense of connection through intimacy, friendship or connecting with ourselves and through empowering self-love, but we can also meet the need for love in a disempowering way by being full of self-pity. Our problems can be an opportunity to connect with ourselves in a 'poor me' way and, along with meeting our needs for significance and certainty, this is perhaps why problems are the greatest addiction in the world today. They meet our needs, but unfortunately in an unhelpful way that stops us experiencing the joy for which we have so much potential as a human being.

By taking time to genuinely connect with and love the many aspects of ourselves, we can also meet this need. When we are connected to our self in the truest sense, this connection naturally aligns with and permeates out as a genuine connection and love for others. To give true love you have to feel true love for yourself. The core of most personal development books is this need to love and appreciate yourself first. We looked in Step 1 at how unique and extraordinary we all are. When we love and appreciate ourselves, we're better able to love and appreciate others. To feel love, be that love which you want to feel.

These first four needs – certainty, variety/uncertainty, love/connection and significance – are the four needs of the personality and we all find ways to meet these, but there are two other needs of our spirit. Although not everyone meets these, they are the doorways to our deeper sense of true happiness and ultimate fulfilment in life. Without meeting these in helpful positive ways, our life will always feel like something is missing.

5. The Need for Growth

For every living thing on Earth to survive and thrive, it must grow. The universe is expanding, and life is part of the universe, so growth and expansion of ourselves is essential to be aligned and feel fulfilled. Whether it's a microorganism, a plant, a relationship, or a creative venture, anything that ceases to grow will stagnate and die. The need for growth both relies on and feeds the first four needs, breathing life into all areas of our existence and as with all our needs, the ways we try and meet this need can be positive or negative for the quality of our life.

For example, growing and expanding can be very fulfilling in its own right but sometimes striving to fulfil this need obsessively can cause us to limit ourselves from being fully present in life, or to postpone applying our growth and knowledge in the world for fear of not being 'ready' or 'enough'. However, fulfilling our need for growth comes with an acceptance that growth is a journey, not a destination, and that continual growth also means allowing ourselves to be real, to be imperfect and to find authentic ways to share what we discover and learn with others. Growth is a never-ending journey and if you as a person are not growing, you are simply not going to experience real fulfilment in your life.

When we develop and grow emotionally, intellectually and spiritually, we become more, and we also will have more value to give and more to contribute.

"Who looks outside, dreams: who looks inside, awakes."– Carl Jung

6. The Need for Contribution

This is the need to give, to care beyond ourselves and is what Maslow referred to when he updated his hierarchy of needs to explain that the self only finds its actualisation in giving to some higher outside goal, in what he called altruism. Our need for contribution comes from a fundamental yearning to have our lives mean something, to make a difference, to give or bring something to the world that continues to benefit others when we are gone. Our need for contribution can be fulfilled in many ways, from volunteering, to simply pausing from our busy day to smile, hug or help someone in need.

The challenge with this human need is that once we connect to the power of being in genuine service to the world, we can quite quickly become overwhelmed with all of the places, people and animals that are in need of support. Many people who value the need for contribution above all others also find it difficult to contribute and give to themselves. Contribution, however, comes not only from what we 'do', but from who we are 'being'. When we are empowered to meet our need for contribution in the simplest of ways, we are aligned with the universe and we feel fulfilled. Life is really about creating meaning and meaning doesn't come from what you get, it comes from what you *give.*

"No one has ever become poor by giving." – Anne Frank

How are you prioritising your needs?

You should now have a good understanding of the six human needs that are inbuilt in all of us. The big practical questions to ask are: How you are prioritising these needs and how are you trying to meet them? Robbins believes your direction in life will largely be determined by which are your top two needs, so let's start by making sure you know which ones they are.

EXERCISE 36
Which Needs Are Your Priority?

Now you understand about human needs and how they drive us to do the things we do, which needs do you think have been the main drivers you in your life until now?

Write along the top of a piece of paper the top six human needs that we all have within us:

Certainty
Variety
Significance
Connection
Growth
Contribution

Underneath this list, draw a vertical line down the middle to split the rest of the page in two.

On the left side of the line, write down the order in which you think you have been prioritising meeting your needs. There is no right or wrong answer in this exercise; the only thing that matters is that you are honest with yourself. It's your life, and honesty is the fastest way to making a better life. It doesn't have to be exact and you may find your priorities change in different circumstances.

When you have done this, circle the top two needs on your list.

Remember, you're trying to meet all six of your needs so don't get too weighed down interrogating your list. It's likely you'll know instinctively which two have been your priority needs anyway.

We all have all human needs, and it's bringing into our conscious awareness those which have been leading us that can start significant change in our life.

Now on the right side of the page, create your new list of priorities and circle the new top two needs which you're going to prioritise in the future.

Robbins believes focusing on the top two needs explains a lot about the choices we make in life. In society today, significance and certainty tend to be reinforced as the most important needs and it's no surprise that these are often the top two needs for most people. Look at your needs and the top two you have identified. Ask yourself how having these at the top has affected the choices you have made in your life so far. By being more aware, you can decide to change your top two needs so you can travel in a new, more fulfilling direction in life. It's not always easy to change quickly as your needs system is deeply programmed, but by starting with awareness you are making the first critical step.

Having your top needs as growth and contribution will give you the greatest sense of fulfilment in life. Contribution is really a form of love, and connecting with others and feeding your spirit will make you feel fulfilled in ways that trying to be certain or significant never well. This is consistent with most of the needs theories we mentioned earlier in the chapter.

Look at those around you; it's likely the most genuinely happy people you know have love, growth and contribution as their top needs, and the least happy usually have significance and certainty as their top two needs.

If you think about some of the great spiritual leaders such as Mahatma Gandhi, Mother Theresa and the Dalai Lama, for example, they have devoted most of their lives to contribution and altruism. Often, it's a change in life, or a big circumstance, that causes people to reflect internally and change focus to wanting to fulfil their human need for contribution above all others. The good news is you can make a change in the priority of your needs anytime once you're aware, and you can practice and reinforce this change until it becomes habitual.

How are you meeting your needs?

When you understand that your top needs are very much shaping your life, the next step is to be aware of how you are meeting them and whether this is empowering and enhancing your life or whether you are sabotaging yourself. Meeting your needs in healthy ways is a critical part of the system for creating an outstanding life.

> *"Everyone experiences the same six human needs. However, everyone finds different ways of satisfying these needs. Each of these needs can be met in ways that are positive or negative. Some ways of satisfying these needs are good for the person, good for others, and good for society, and some are bad for everyone."* – *Cloé Madanes*

EXERCISE 37
How Have You Been Meeting Your Needs?

On a clean sheet of paper, write down the ways you believe you have been meeting each need, based on your list from Exercise 36.

For example, to meet the need for significance you might have been buying things in the hope others will think of you in a certain way. A car, a personalised number plate, a handbag, a branded piece of clothing, a watch. In this exercise, honesty is definitely your fastest route to a better life. There's no point in pretending; you can't bullshit yourself.

Spend a chunk of time on this exercise and write down anything that comes into your mind about each need and your behaviour in meeting that need.

The purpose is not to have an exhaustive list but to stimulate your thinking and awareness in this area so you can start to make more effective choices of ways you can meet these needs.

Meeting your need for significance by looking for validation from others, and meeting your need for certainty by trying to control everything, won't make you happy. If you're trying to look good all the time for others, you'll not only feel an emptiness inside, but if you are constantly comparing yourself to others there are always going to be people who have more or are 'better' than you against whatever criteria you are measuring. And it's impossible to always have certainty, as life is uncertain. The only certainty is the certainty you bring from within you. In Step 5 we will look at the importance of having a clear sense of purpose for your life, and you'll see how this links in many ways to contribution, growth and love.

If you meet three or more of your human needs with a behaviour, that behaviour will likely become addictive, so we need to make extra sure we're meeting our needs in positive ways. One of the biggest ways to sabotage yourself in your life is through self-pity and telling yourself how unfortunate you are or how you are a victim. We know from Step 2 and 3 that seeing yourself as a victim is not helpful and that there are more empowering ways to look at everything that happens in your life. We discussed how taking responsibility for your life experience is critical and that while we can't control much of what happens, we can always control the meanings we give.

However, the reason self-pity and 'poor me' thinking can become a far-too-frequented emotional home for many is that it simply meets some of your human needs, and usually at least three. It can make you feel significant to have 'problems', you can connect with yourself when you feel the victim, and this kind of thinking can give you certainty as you know the feeling so well. The challenge is to become aware of what is happening, and to see that the way you are meeting your needs is unhelpful. Thinking we have problems is a very popular pastime, as it meets our needs, but meeting our needs in a healthier way will make us feel much happier. Try and meet your need for significance, for example, by being a positive force in the world, and meet your need for certainty from your inner strength and knowledge that you can always control your response.

> *"The ultimate significance in life comes not from something external, but from something internal. It comes from a sense of esteem for ourselves, which is not something we can ever get from someone else. People can tell you you're beautiful, smart, intelligent, the best, or they can tell you that you are the most horrible human being on Earth—but what matters is what you think about yourself. Whether or not you believe that deep inside you are continuing to grow and push yourself, to do and give more than was comfortable or you even thought possible." – Tony Robbins.*

Let's look at drug-taking as a behaviour example. The reason people take drugs – apart from making them feel good temporarily – is to meet their 'needs'. Unfortunately, these needs are likely to be met in destructive ways. If the drug-taking meets three or more needs, the experience often becomes highly addictive, notwithstanding any physical addiction. Drug-taking has a huge negative impact on society and the problem is growing. Trying to stop supply isn't working. It will only be in reducing demand and reducing people's desire to take drugs that the issue will be more successfully addressed. When people realise they can make themselves feel great naturally and meet their needs without the negative impacts, recreational drug use will become much less prevalent.

Having money can meet your human needs as it can give you certainty, allow you variety, and it can make you feel significant, but how you view it and use it will determine whether you meet your needs in positive or negative ways. What about love? Money might buy you sex but true love cannot be bought, and money often attracts unhealthy relationships. Money can buy you learning and you can give it away but if you value significance above all else, money will leave you empty, unless it comes from a contribution you've made.

"I've seen it a million times–people can equate their net worth with their self-worth. Their identity is married so deeply to their bank statements and quarterly portfolio reports that they've forgotten that money is simply a vehicle for trying to meet our needs." – Tony Robbins

If you can orientate yourself to focus on your needs of growth, contribution and love and if you find ways to meet these needs positively to make that behaviour addictive, you will feel depths of fulfilment that are so much more joyful than temporary fixes of pleasure.

Achievement and fulfilment

In Western society, we're generally encouraged to be achievers and achievement is seen as the high marker of success. We celebrate people who we identify as having made great achievements and this is commendable in many ways and has a huge part to play for society and for the individual, but 'achievement' and 'fulfilment' are very different. Most of us are striving for achievements in our life. We have goals for our career, our finances, and the possessions we want, and achievement in this sense is just a science. It follows certain steps and if we apply the steps, we'll increase the probability of 'achieving'. However, for all the achieving and all the progress we have made as human beings, we seem to be unhappier than ever. Statistics on depression and unhappiness show no precise link to money or material achievement, and we regularly hear about the high-flying career executive, business person or celebrity who seemingly has everything they wanted to achieve, but who is deeply unhappy and 'depressed'.

"The world is becoming increasingly materialistic, and mankind is reaching toward the very zenith of external progress, driven by an insatiable desire for power and vast possessions. Yet by this vain striving for perfection in a world where everything is relative, they wander even further away from inward peace and happiness of the mind." – Dalai Lama

If you search the internet for famous people who have killed themselves, you may be surprised just how many people, who seemed to have so much, decided to check out of the living experience early. The lists show far too many people who had achieved what they had set out to achieve, financially and famously, but who were desperately unhappy. Instead of bringing them happiness and freedom, being sought-after, rich and at the top of their game lead to questioning their self-worth, and a realisation that achievement itself does not make you feel fulfilled. Whether it was Avicii, Marilyn Monroe, Robin Williams, Kurt Cobain, Brian Jones, L'Wren Scott, Jimi Hendrix or Alexander McQueen, or any number of other famous people, they all believed the pain of living was not worth carrying on.

This is desperately sad and a tragic way to end any life, but of course these are just the famous people, and there are many, many, many more people not in the public eye who have killed themselves because they didn't feel fulfilled. Most suicides don't make the headlines, but each life ended is equally tragic. We've looked already at the statistics from the World Health Organisation which reveal that every 40 seconds someone takes their own life, and shockingly these numbers are predicted to get worse. There has never been a greater need for a system people can follow to sort themselves out.

Our children are often programmed with a model of what success is like and then they either achieve it and realise that this alone doesn't make them feel fulfilled, or they don't achieve and feel they have failed. We urgently need to teach our children – and everyone else – that achievement without fulfilment is a failure in living.

What you get will never make you sustainably happy and fulfilled. What you become will. And at the heart of this 'becoming more' is understanding our human needs and how we are meeting them. Achievement is a science, whereas fulfilment is an art, but we aren't taught about this art. The art lies in understanding the keys to fulfilment, and rather than seeking to have more, that it is richer to 'be more'. The world is full of many achievers who are miserable and it's the feeling of being fulfilled, of feeling really alive and full of joy, that is to be really successful, yet we focus our teaching mainly around the science of achievement. However, by following the SYSO System, you can commit to making the most of your life, having an experience of both achievement and fulfilment and in full knowledge that they are not mutually exclusive. In fact, they can be mutually reinforcing.

When I got really honest with myself and started on my own journey of personal development, I realised my top two needs had been significance and variety. I wanted to achieve but I also wanted to feel special and be recognised, and I craved variety and stimulation. Now with awareness and practice, my priorities have changed and my top needs are now growth and contribution. Moreover, I'm meeting these in healthier ways and my life feels so much more fulfilled. I have always felt grateful and happy in life, and much thanks to my wonderful parents for the upbringing and programming, but I thought even more achievement would bring even greater levels of happiness. It feels good to achieve, of course, but I was achieving with a focus on meeting my needs for significance and variety. I knew something was missing, even if I didn't know exactly what or why.

Seeking deeper fulfilment in your life rather than short-term unsustainable pleasure boosts, having a purpose bigger than yourself, and focusing on growing and giving, will transform your experience. This is indeed the secret to living, which is entirely consistent with Maslow's work later in life and at the very heart of Tony Robbins' teachings.

"I can understand wanting to have a million dollars... but once you get beyond that, I have to tell you it's the same hamburger." – Bill Gates

EXERCISE 38
Review Your Needs

Make an audit before you go to sleep of some of the things you did today and which needs they met.

For example, how much of what you did today was because of what you wanted others to think of you? Be completely honest. That is how you will make the greatest changes to your experience of life.

You can make notes as a checklist or just work through it in your mind. The important thing is to become more aware of your needs, and how you are prioritising and meeting them.

It might feel complicated or confusing to start with, but just start. Even if you initially think of a couple of examples of how you met one need. You can build on this and the idea is to think about how you met each of your needs.

Find a way of remembering the six needs. Write them down, make notes on your phone or whatever you need to help remember these innate human needs you have of certainty, variety, significance, connection, growth and contribution.

"If you make music for the human needs you have within yourself, then you do it for all humans who need the same things. You enrich humanity with the profound expression of these feelings." – Billy Joel

STEP 5
Have a Clear Philosophy About the Purpose of Your life

"The best way to find yourself is to lose yourself in the service of others." – Mahatma Gandhi

There are things about life which it seems wise to accept that we cannot understand while we are alive. Letting go and being comfortable with this uncertainty can be liberating, lightening and can dramatically increase the quality of our lives. Knowing we don't know invites us to trust in life, trust in that which created you, whatever you believe 'that' to be. 'Something' wanted you to exist. You were chosen to be. Trust the process, give it up to God, the universe, the source, or whatever you believe about the higher power that chose you to be. It is stressful to always need to be certain about your life and in control, and it's also not that attractive for those around you if you're uptight, controlling and craving certainty. Let go, breathe deeply, smile, feel your aliveness and simply appreciate being and that you were chosen. Every moment is a special occasion, a one-time only life event and a gift. Become more aware, appreciate more deeply, and you will transform your experience of life.

Our only real certainty is what happens at the end of being alive which for everyone, of course, is death. Although we don't know what happens after, we do know that life was here long before we were born and life will likely go on long after we die. Life goes on but we – the individual in our body form – don't, and life therefore is about more than just our life. This may well be an unwelcome shock to many, but life isn't just about you! It is about you, but it's not all about you.

Our place in time

So, if life is not just about you, or me, or any individual life, what does it all mean? What is our purpose of being here, especially when we consider that our time here is for such a relatively very short period in all of time? Think about how much life has gone before us, and that which seems likely will follow us, and keep in perspective how your life is a small, but essential, part of all life.

EXERCISE 39
Keep Time in Perspective

On a piece of paper, draw a line representing all of time. Time that has been and which likely will be. It could be argued that time is infinite, but have a start and ending to your line just for this exercise.

Now on the line you have drawn, mark a section that represents your estimated living time on this whole line of life. Of course, it's going to be a tiny section, or more like a tiny dot depending on how you marked it.

The idea isn't to spook you as to how little time that seems, but rather to help build your awareness and keep perspective that life was here long before us and life will likely be here long after us. Life goes on, but we in this form don't.

We are alive for only a fraction of the total life line, but we are all incredibly important in the role we play. We are dependent on the past, we influence the future and without individual life, there is no collective life. Every expression of life is an essential part of the whole. We are all VIPs and everything we do affects more than just us.

At the time of writing, the average life expectancy in the UK is just over 79 years for men and around 83 years for women. Worldwide, it's 68 for men and 73 for women. In Japan, which has the highest life expectancy of any country, men currently live an average of 81 years, and women 87 years. That's 4524 weeks, or 31,777 days, if you happen to be a Japanese woman. Of course, the age at which you die will depend on a lot of factors and people do die unexpectedly at all ages. Even if you manage to live to the age of the oldest person who has ever lived, which as of today is 122 years and 164 days, and even with the developments in anti-ageing and longevity treatments, the life of an individual is still a very, very, very short time in the whole time of life.

"Time is long but life is short." – Stevie Wonder

Our home, Earth, is thought to be a little over 4.5 billion years old, and life itself is believed to have originated here around 3.8 billion years ago with tiny individual cells of bacteria. About 2.8 billion years ago, there were multicellular forms of life and only in the last 570 million years did the kinds of life forms we're familiar with begin to evolve. Mammals are thought not to have existed until about 200 million years ago and we as humans, or Homo sapiens, are only about 200,000 years old.

And this is just looking at the time that has passed. The more time that passes in the future, the more of a small flicker our life will be. Of course, we don't know how much more life will follow; will it carry on infinitely or will there be an end to life as we know it and if so, when?

Life is precious and fragile

In the last a couple of billion years, life has survived being frozen, battered by rocks from space, mass poisoning and disease, and even lethal radiation. It does seem difficult to completely wipe out life on this planet, but there are plenty of potential threats. Probably the nearest life has come to ultimate destruction was 250 million years ago, during the End-Permian mass extinction when volcanic activity destroyed around 85% of all species living on land, and 95% of all marine species, but life hung on and evolved again. About 450 million years ago, it's believed that plant roots broke up bedrock into soil, speeding up the chemical reaction between minerals in the rocks and carbon dioxide in the atmosphere which weakened the greenhouse effect, triggering the ice age.

Scientists are studying many of the current risks including, for example, stray asteroids, or planets colliding. If a massive asteroid could contribute to the extinction of all of the world's large dinosaurs, could one also wipe out all life on Earth? Could it be that other planets were made lifeless by intense waves of gamma-ray radiation from explosions or collisions in space, and that these types of gamma ray bursts still have the potential to destroy Earth's ozone layer, exposing life to deadly ultraviolet radiation from the sun? Astronomers are monitoring a number of stars that could potentially be on a collision course with our solar system, although predicting their exact journey is impossible and it's unlikely that there is any immediate threat.

The sun, of course, is our source of light, and energy for almost all the life on Earth, but it is also gradually getting hotter and some scientists believe that it eventually could be hot enough to evaporate all the oceans, send temperatures soaring and wipe out all but the most resistant microorganisms. And humans aren't helping! Modern humans are believed to be different from all earlier species in that we are self-consciously intelligent. But with destructive environmental behaviour, ballooning global population and threats of nuclear war, are we really that intelligent? Unless humans make some radical changes, Earth might actually be destroyed by its current occupants and life's biggest threat could be self-destruction.

There are clearly a variety of risks that could wipe out life, and maybe others that we don't know about, but the good news is that most are highly unlikely and should be a long, long way into the future, by which time we might have colonised another planet or evolved our expertise to deal with these or other potential threats anyway. As humans, we may be the greatest threat to ourselves but we may also be the greatest saviours. Let's hope so. In any case, Steven Hawking thinks we will be fine for at least another 20 billion years!

None of this is written to cause alarm, but rather to help us keep in perspective how much life there has been, likely will be and that our living experience is only a tiny flicker of uncertainty in time. Life is precious, but it also precarious, and increased awareness of our brevity and fragility should help us appreciate the gift that is our time alive.

"What we normally describe as history doesn't interest me. It's a constraint." – David Christian

Your unique contribution

Life goes on but the individual does not, and life, therefore, is not *all* about us. It is about us but not all about us. There is so much more than just our life. Rather than feeling that our individual lives are therefore relatively insignificant, we should instead appreciate that we have a critical role, and a huge potential, to make an infinite contribution to the greater whole which we are all a part of. The whole is only the whole because of the parts, because of each of us. Without an awareness of this bigger picture and without a clear philosophy for our purpose here, it could easily feel like it doesn't matter how we live as we'll soon be gone. However, when we understand that all of life is interconnected (Step 6) and that we have an impact that goes far beyond each of us infinitely, we can become acutely aware that every life is absolutely critical in the role it plays to the whole of life.

"Everything in the universe has a purpose. Indeed, the invisible intelligence that flows through everything in a purposeful fashion is also flowing through you." – Wayne Dye

When we understand the contribution our life makes to the whole of life, and when we have a clear philosophy about the purpose of our life, we can feel liberated, valuable and comfortable with uncertainty.

We will also feel most content when we are being the best version of the person we are capable of being. For example, if we were designed to be a light it would be our shining and illuminating which would make us feel useful and content, doing that which we were designed to do as best we can. Our experience would be optimised and we would be at our most valuable.

Life is about you and lighting yourself up, but it is also about your impact and how you can illuminate other life. Changing your perspective in this way will change your life and we should always remind ourselves what a special gift it is to be alive, but also a responsibility, for ourselves and for other life.

The 'wow' of the everyday

Living is a special occasion and should call for regular celebration. Most people feel a sense of 'wow' when they see a beautiful sunset or a full moon, but what if we felt a sense of wow about everyday things in life too? When we orientate ourselves to feeling 'wow' at the sight of a tree, at a bird singing, the touch of water running over our hands, the taste of our favourite fruit, or the smell of a beautiful flower, when we start to appreciate the beauty and wonder all around us, we can start to feel deeply even more grateful that we are here now as something so miraculous and amazing and as part of the whole.

> *"There are two great days in a person's life – the day we are born and the day we discover why." – William Barclay*

Without this sense of perspective and without understanding our purpose and direction, how can we know what to do with our life? What direction to take? How to evaluate how well we are living? Having a clear philosophy about the purpose of your life, understanding you are here to enjoy yourself AND contribute to life, will instead give you the biggest source of strength, certainty and feeling of aliveness.

If I get into my car but don't know why or where I am going, then I'm probably going to quickly feel frustrated and lost. In life, unfortunately, many people feel frustrated and lost because they simply lack clarity about why and where they are going, or the purpose of their life. Most people just 'idle' on their programmed beliefs, seeking pleasure and avoiding pain, but without a clear sense of purpose, life can feel hollow and like something is missing.

When we are living without realising our potential to benefit life beyond ourselves, we will always feel an emptiness. It can also be quite scary as death approaches, if you don't have a philosophy that includes the greater sense of your life as an essential part of all life. If the ultimate source of anxiety is fear of and uncertainty about the future, we do know for sure that the future ends in death for each of us in the form we are now. Death is the only certainty.

Facing up to death

Facing up to death, accepting its inevitability, and integrating it into a life philosophy that starts with how useful we are to other life while we are here, will help us make the most of the gift of our time alive. As humans, we have the capacity to think consciously, and ask questions about death and why we are here. This could be what separates humans from other forms of life, although we can't be sure. Do dogs, cats and fish wonder about their existence, their purpose, their consciousness? We don't know and it could be that there are many other aspects of thought and consciousness in the living realm beyond just human capabilities.

Purpose of any kind gives us focus and helps us feel alive. A powerful example of the importance of having a clear purpose can be seen in Holocaust survivor Viktor Frankl's famous book, *Man's Search for Meaning*, in which he describes his horrific experiences in concentration camps during the Second World War. Frankl saw that the inmates who were most likely to survive were those who felt they had a goal or purpose. Frankl himself spent a lot of time trying to reconstruct a manuscript of his life's work which he had lost on his journey to the camp. Others held on to a vision of their future, such as seeing their family again or a major task to complete once they were free. Frankl's conclusion is that, with purpose and clear reason, humans can survive much physical and emotional trauma.

"Life is never made unbearable by circumstances, but only by lack of meaning." – Viktor Frankl

Finding your purpose has long been a main focus in personal development approaches and there are numerus books on this topic alone. Religious texts such as the Bible, for example, are often thought of as the first and most significant teachings on meaning and purpose in life, but there has been much theorising about human purpose since life began, and many interpretations over the years.

In around 400BC, the Greek school of philosophy, the Cyrenaics, believed the only real goal in life should be pleasure in the present and people should do what makes them happy in the moment instead of planning for an uncertain future. Mohism, on the other hand, a philosophical movement in China around the same time, argued that everyone should be treated equally, that we should help each other and that rewards come in the afterlife.

At the extreme end of philosophy on life's meaning, nihilists believe there is no point in a person's existence and destruction is the only thing that had any sort of purpose. In contrast, Tibetan philosophy preaches one major goal in life; to end the world's suffering which comes only through understanding and evolving ourselves. The Epicureans believed everything to be made up of tiny particles, including the human body's soul. They suggested that we need to come to terms with death as we're not able to control it, and that behaving in a good and honourable manner is vital to feeling pleasure, as guilt and anxiety can eat away at us if we don't.

For the Aztecs, the ultimate meaning of life is to live in balance with nature and allow the continuation of the energy force called Teotl that gives rise to the next generation. Humanists don't believe there is any specific meaning of life at all and they believe that human experience and rational thinking provide the only source of both knowledge and a moral code to live by.

Aristotle believed happiness to be the central purpose of human life, and he believed we should focus on physical and mental wellbeing. He introduced the science of happiness in a classical sense and he thought that our happiness was dependent on ourselves rather than others. For Aristotle, happiness is really to be looked at as how well you lived up to your human potential and over your whole life.

> *"One swallow does not a summer make, nor one fine day; similarly, one day or brief time of happiness does not make a person entirely happy." – Aristotle*

Aristotle also believed happiness is really an activity of the soul and that lacking willpower and pursuing short term pleasure can lead to long-term pain, whereas postponing gratification for a deeper happiness is a more fulfilling path. Albert Einstein, when asked about his belief on the meaning of life, said it was simply: "To create satisfaction for ourselves and for other people." Auguste Comte coined the term altruism, as the opposite of egoism, and proposed that our purpose as humans is to be selfless as opposed to selfish.

These are just some of the more prominent theories, and there have been many more, but the key question is really how can we use any theory in terms of practical application to our own living experience? Some theories suggest we sacrifice our own pleasure for the pursuit of others and yet some propose living life for yourself.

Be a beacon of happy

The SYSO System is based on both, focusing on enjoying yourself AND on being the best contributor you can. These are actually both mutually reinforcing, as by pursuing a life of contribution you will get the feelings of happiness and joy from that. When you feel really happy and full of joy in your life, you are likely to be the best contributor to other lives. Perhaps the best way to think about how to reach your fullest potential for fulfilment is to think of yourself as being a beacon of happy, rather than a receiver of happy.

> *"This is the true joy in life, the being used for a purpose recognized by yourself as a mighty one; the being thoroughly worn out before you are thrown on the scrap heap; the being a force of Nature instead of a feverish selfish little clod of ailments and grievances complaining that the world will not devote itself to making you happy." – George Bernard Shaw*

Many self-improvement books talk about finding our unique purpose, or the special 'something' that we are born to do with our lives. However, instead of thinking about finding a unique purpose for ourselves, the SYSO System suggests it's more helpful to focus on the main purpose we all have, the bigger purpose of all human life. Once we clearly understand that bigger picture, there are many ways we can live a fulfilling life within that. Apart from also putting much less pressure on ourselves to find the 'one special thing we were born to do', we can stay open to creating the life we want when maybe we have lots of passions and purposes rather than just one?

However, the big question: 'What is the purpose of human life' can seem overwhelming. Religion has long been the main guide for many, with narratives, symbols and traditions that are intended to give meaning to life. According to some estimates, there are around 4200 religions in the world and nearly 75% of the world's population practices one of the five most influential religions: Buddhism, Christianity, Hinduism, Islam or Judaism. Christianity and Islam together are estimated to cover the religious affiliation of more than half of the world's population. Over 80% of all living humans are subscribed to beliefs in the form of organised religious belief systems, and while the religiously unaffiliated have grown globally, many of these 'nonbelievers' still have some form of religious-type beliefs based on their cultural programming. Organised religion is humanity's biggest programming machine and has been our biggest source of theory on meaning and purpose, but it has also been the cause of much conflict and confusion.

Some religious doctrines suggest that our purpose is to find happiness, to love others, to become the best version of ourselves, to follow God's will, or all of these, and there is much merit in many of these theories. However, it seems there often isn't real clarity about our purpose in the highest, simplest, purest sense. With the SYSO System, which is concerned with practical applications, we think there is a much simpler way to look at this question without it being a cumbersome topic to dance around or avoid. Your clear philosophy on the purpose of your life should be your compass for everything, for the direction you take in your life and against which you can evaluate your time here. If you work for a successful business, for example, you'll no doubt clearly know the purpose of the business, which is usually to make money by selling products or services. If you join a gym, you'll have a clear purpose for doing that, and if you choose to book a holiday, you have a clear purpose about why and where you would like to go. Our life is no different; we need to have a clear purpose about what we are doing here, or there will always be a confusing void in our life.

"Giving back is as good for you as it is for those you are helping, because giving gives you purpose. When you have a purpose-driven life, you're a happier person." – Goldie Hawn

If everything is just about us, life won't be fulfilling, and that's not why we are here. If it's always about others, with no joy for ourselves, it will seem unbalanced and we won't be realising the gift of our human experience. So, in simple terms it's about both. It's about being happy *and* contributing. These are mutually reinforcing and the highest purpose of all life is to be useful to, and supporting of, other life. By being useful to other life, you'll feel fulfilled and happy which are the feelings we are trying to feel, whatever philosophy we have.

Usefulment

The SYSO System suggests a new word to describe the target for a happy and fulfilled life. This word is 'usefulment', which is the feeling of fulfilment we experience by feeling our life is of use. We have already said life isn't just about each of us, and by being useful we're not acting just for ourselves. But we've also said life is about you and we shouldn't think of being useful and being happy as two separate things.

"The purpose of life is to enjoy and make the most of your own life while being useful and making the most impact on other life." – The SYSO System

The key point of this chapter is that life goes on and we in our human form don't, and so the impact of our life should be measured in terms of the impact on other life. It has to be about more than just living for yourself, and if you look for evidence of the most fulfilled and sustainably happy people, you will likely notice a trend; they tend to be orientated to what they can do for others. About 80 years of living, if we are fortunate, is a 'long time' in many ways to be alive, and we can experience so much in that length of life, but our own living has to be about more than just the time we are alive. Everything is more than the individual part and we are all more than our individual life. We are all interconnected (Step 6).

"Inter-dependence, of course, is a fundamental law of nature. Not only higher forms of life but also many of the smallest insects are social beings who, without any religion, law or education, survive by mutual cooperation based on an innate recognition of their interconnectedness. The subtlest level of material phenomena is also governed by interdependence. All phenomena from the planet we inhabit; from the oceans and clouds to the forests and flowers that surround us, arise in dependence upon subtle patterns of energy. Without their proper interaction, they dissolve and decay." – Dalai Lama

We were created because of events prior to our own birth, which happened because of events prior to those, and events prior to those and so on. We have an effect that carries on long after our time alive on Earth through the impact we have on others, who have impact on others and so on. Our life is about much more than just our time alive; it's about something bigger than ourselves. When we start to tune into and build deep awareness from that perspective, we orientate ourselves to the impact our life can have on other life and in doing so we will feel much more fulfilled, aligned and deeply grounded.

Your life purpose

In the SYSO System, the purpose of life is the impact we can make on other lives while at the same time enjoying our own life. That's it. Your life purpose isn't more complicated than that and shouldn't be a heavy load for you to overthink or try and figure out. How you live in heading towards that overriding objective is now up to you, to create a life in line with what you enjoy and what you can do that is useful.

> *"When I went to school, they asked me what I wanted to be when I grew up. I wrote down happy. They told me I didn't understand the assignment. I told them they didn't understand life." – John Lennon*

If you're spending your life doing things you don't enjoy and not making a contribution to life, you'll feel something is missing and that you're not fully alive. Think about enjoying life *and* contributing to other life, not either/or. Contributing to life beyond ourselves provides a great sense of enjoyment or fulfilment and the more we are enjoying life, the more likely we are to make others feel good and be the best contributor. It is mutually reinforcing like the pattern of all life.

Scientific research provides compelling data to support the theory that *giving* is a powerful pathway to personal growth and lasting happiness. Through brain scanning technology, we now know that giving activates the same parts of the brain that are stimulated by food and sex, and experiments show evidence that being of service to others is hardwired in the brain.

Helping others may just be the secret to living a life that is not only happier but also healthier. Giving releases endorphins in much the same way that exercise does and the 'rush' that people sometimes experience after performing an altruistic act has been referred to as 'helper's high'. Giving can also help you feel more grateful for what you have in your own life, as good deeds are often done for those who have more challenging life circumstances to deal with, which can serve to remind us that our own lives are actually really good.

> *"For it is in giving that we receive." – St Francis of Assisi*

Now we have a clear articulation and philosophy for what our life is about, we can measure the success of living in terms of the impact we have on other lives, and the enjoyment we have while impacting. Growing and giving as the secret to living, and focusing on this mantra, will lead us on a path of deeper fulfillment in life. Achieving is really a science, or steps to follow, whereas fulfillment as we looked at in Step 4 can be considered much more of an art. We now have the 'how' of this art, by focusing on a life of usefulment. Generally, when you ask people what the meaning and purpose of their life is, their answers will be complex, but it isn't really that complicated. Enjoy yourself and help others. That's all you need to focus on. That is your purpose.

> *"If you want happiness for an hour, take a nap. If you want happiness for a day, go fishing. If you want happiness for a year, inherit a fortune. If you want happiness for a lifetime, help somebody." – Chinese proverb*

Some might ask; once I focus on the contribution my life can have on other lives, what is the purpose above that? Why does life exist at all? But what if you let go of that question and instead accept that you aren't going to get that answer in this lifetime? Give it up to that which created you and trust in the process. Focus on the purpose of you being useful to life and the feeling that gives you.

If you're still not convinced, think about alternative philosophies you could have, such as just living for yourself, a winner takes all attitude, or a belief that everything is a battle and screw everyone else. Or at the other extreme, giving everything to others without considering yourself at all. In all of these philosophies, you are going to be unfulfilled. The first three approaches will leave you spiritually empty and the other one will leave you exhausted and just as empty, as you'll have failed to look after yourself.

Practise living a life where you know that everything you do goes beyond you, and the value you can have impacting other life. Everything you do is important.

> *"Act as if what you do makes a difference. It does." – William James*

Commit today, if you haven't already, to your new simple and clear philosophy about life, which will guide you in everything you do. Think about the ripple effect of all your actions and make sure you're crystal clear about this new, clearly defined purpose. Write it down, put it on a Post-it note and keep checking in against this to assess how you are doing. Ask if what you are doing at any time is aligned with your purpose? Ask yourself how you can have more fun and more positive impact on others? Without your clear purpose, without knowing where you're going, you can't go anywhere worth going! With a clear direction, you should feel amazing – growing and experiencing the secret of joyful living.

EXERCISE 40
Know Your Purpose

Write down your purpose:

"My purpose is to enjoy life and help others."

Say it really clearly.

Say it loudly and repeatedly, as an affirmation like we did in Step 2.

Check in with yourself at the end of every day for 30 days. Score yourself on a scale of 1–10 how you lived that day in alignment with your purpose.

Ask yourself your two purpose questions:

1. Am I enjoying myself?
2. Am I contributing?

Celebrate your giving and become more aware of the gift of the feeling that is giving.

Stick a copy of your written purpose, your life slogan, where you can see it – on your computer as your screensaver, on your dashboard, on a mirror.

This as your 'satnav destination' and the journey will be amazing!

"My purpose is to enjoy life and help others."

Once you take the focus of your life away from it being just about you, to being about you so you can be about others, you'll feel different. You'll radiate calm and contentment, people will experience you differently and sense your certainty in life. You will be your most self-assured and it will show, radiating out from you as an authentic human beacon of being.

When you have purpose, you have a place to aim, a clear target, and you can then set all your life goals in alignment for this greater purpose. Even after digesting what has been written here, and some of the deliberate repetition, just do a quick bullshit check. Does your purpose statement feel right to you?

Identify your passions

Pursuing your passions doesn't have to be selfish. When you have a clear philosophy for the purpose of your life, your passions should align with your reason for being. In Japanese there is a word, *ikigai*, which describes a way of thinking about your passions which can be helpful. Ikigai is composed of 2 words; *iki* meaning life and *gai* meaning the realisation of hopes and expectations.

There are four elements in ikigai, usually represented as circles, where the idea is to find where they all overlap. Think about what you love (your passion), what the world needs (your mission), what you are good at (your vocation) and what you can get paid for (your profession) and what delivers against all four of those. Ikigai is seen as the source of value or what makes one's life truly worthwhile, and using this framework can help you decide what you're going to focus your time on when creating the life you want within the context of your bigger purpose and quest for usefulment.

"Life isn't about finding yourself. Life is about creating yourself." – George Bernard Shaw

Whatever our passions, we should strive to live usefully and think of our life not as trying to get as much as we can for ourselves, but rather an exercise in becoming more so we can give more. You don't have to strive to live like Mother Teresa, but there are always higher levels of spiritual enlightenment and growth we can strive for. When we have a positive impact on others, we get a boost of endorphins which are natural happy chemicals, and when we're happy, we're much more fun to be around, which will make others happy. The cycle works the other way too, of course, and reinforcing unhappy and selfishness is at the heart of many of society's social problems. A great life really boils down to giving. Giving of your spirit, your kindness, your love, your compassion. This is who you are as a human, this is your natural state to feel great and to be useful.

"We make a living by what we get; we make a life by what we give." – Winston Churchill

Without a clear philosophy for the purpose of your life and without prioritising growth and your contribution to others, life will never feel enough. We live in a time when we have more stuff than ever, great advancements in medicine, technology, travel and communication, but have seemingly never been more unhappy. Antidepressants with $15 billion dollars annual sales are currently the third most frequently taken medication and are generally considered as 'quite normal', even for the mildest of symptoms. Trying to medicate our way out of bad feelings, however, is not sustainable and it messes with our biochemistry in destructive ways long-term.

Perhaps the biggest addiction is our addiction to problems. Having problems can meet several of our human needs as we looked at in Step 4, including bringing us attention and feelings of significance. We have, as a society, become very good at thinking we're victims, practising self-pity and obsessing over ourselves. Far too often we seek attention in unhealthy ways, which can be amplified through the ease, reach and speed of social media, but this can undermine the power we have to take responsibility for the meaning we give, and how we respond to anything that happens in our lives.

Most emotional problems are because we're focused too much on ourselves.

Keep remembering that life isn't just about you, me or any of us. It is about all of us. We are all in the same boat, and others aren't your enemy, even if it might seem like that sometimes. *Keep it light and see life through the lens of fun and giving.* We are a little, but incredibly important, part in the tree of life, and we are all related. Perhaps a better way to look at life is thinking about how you can look after others, your brothers and sisters on the same journey?

> *"It is because our own human existence is so dependent on the help of others that our need for love lies at the very foundation of our existence. Therefore, we need a genuine sense of responsibility and a sincere concern for the welfare of others." – Dalai Lama*

EXERCISE 41
Highlight Your Purpose on Your Vision Board

In Chapter 2 you created your own personal vision board of the life you want. Revisit this board now and write your purpose in big bold letters:

"MY PURPOSE IS TO ENJOY LIFE AND HELP OTHERS."

This is the most important part of your vision board as it sets your overall direction. You can look at all the aspects of the vision you created and ask yourself are there any changes you now need to make, or does everything align perfectly with your new clarity on what your life is about?

Give your smile

Now you have more clarity on your purpose, you will become more consciously aware of how you are living and the impact it has far beyond just yourself. There is a ripple effect in every action and interaction and everything you do or say or think. Recognise your power and take responsibility for being a happy soul. Be kind, judge others by their intentions and realise not everyone has evolved or become conscious to the level you have. Life is for living. By giving you will feel most alive, and there is one thing you can give easily, anytime, and for free; your smile. Give your smile and see how it feels for you and everyone you give it to. When you see someone without a smile, give them yours. This is also your best look as a human.

I was catching an internal flight in the US from Denver airport a few years ago and as my wife handed her boarding pass to the attendant, he checked it, and with his own big smile said to her: "Thank you for sharing that smile." I don't know if that was part of a customer service training initiative but it certainly felt genuine and was a free, instant atmosphere changer that felt good for everyone involved. A simple, free action by someone doing their job had an impact far beyond themselves. What if we thought of ourselves as sharing everything we do, as our behaviour being something that radiates out from us for the benefit of others, as well as affecting how we feel?

"Making money is a happiness; making other people happy is a super-happiness." – Muhammad Yunus

EXERCISE 42
See Your Time in All Time

In Exercise 35 you took a ride in your perspective bubble over your life from birth, and you can jump in your perspective bubble at any time. It is one of the most useful tools and vehicles you have in the garage of your mind.

Let's climb in again. Float up above your life, and with your control stick, slowly move back over your life, looking at the beautiful tapestry of events and people who have led you to where you are.

This time however, when you get to your birth, keep on going.

Let your relaxed mind take you back to wherever it feels natural; to the lives that lead to your life. To your mother's pregnancy, to your birth father, to their lives, and back to when and where they were children and the lives that lead to their lives.

You may have seen photos of your ancestors when they were young which can help to visualise how they were, but it doesn't matter if not, and some people don't know their parents or much about their ancestors at all. That's ok too, just keep going, keep feeling and seeing there was much life before your life.

Even if you don't know the lives before yours, you can see that your life only exists because of many lives before you.

You can go as far back as you want and you can take side journeys into the lives of those who were connected with the lives of the people you are seeing.

Everything is moving and as you float back and through time, you will see clearly just how much life there has been, and how each life is the result of other previous lives and the impact they had.

You can float back and forwards over the time before your birth, and when you are ready to come back to now, just float up even higher and notice all the life before you were born laid out below, all leading to your life now.

You can also look ahead to the amount of life that lies in front of you and think about how the life you create will impact so many other lives.

Finally, bring your bubble back to where you are and slowly descend to the vivid and clear now.

Everything has an impact far beyond ourselves and far beyond the moment. This is the power you have as a human to influence life.

> You are a gift and when you tune into this power and start living as a beacon of fun and usefulness, you will experience new levels of joy and fulfilment knowing that your impact will go on forever.

No one knows what happens when we die, but we do know our bodies are still here after the life energy force has gone. This energy has left your earth body form but it is still in the universe; there is nowhere else for it to go. All the impacts you have had live on, as there is nowhere else for them to go, and they live on in the lives of everyone you touched and the lives of everyone they have touched. When you become more aware of this, you understand and act differently, knowing your life is much more than just the time you are alive on Earth.

Death is not the end

My father died suddenly and unexpectedly on the second green while playing golf on the 6th July 2009 at 9.34 am. A cardiac arrest didn't give him much chance of survival given where he was, at a time when defibrillators were much less prevalent. It certainly was a shock and sad, but I vividly remember two things when I attended the hospital that afternoon with my mother and sisters to identify his body: Firstly, he was still there, in body form, but it was immediately clear that the life force had gone from his body. As I cried, my tears and energy in motion were initially from the realisation his life had passed and thoughts of missing him terribly. But then in a second, vivid realisation, my thoughts turned to how many others his life had touched and I felt a calmness knowing his life hadn't just gone, it lives on always and in everything he touched. It lives on through the impact he had on others and the impact they had on others and so on.

My father nearly died seven years earlier and had major heart surgery. As he recovered, I remember him saying he thought he must have other useful things to do, now that he had been given more time alive. His life wasn't just about him and it isn't just about me, or my mum, or my sisters, or his friends, or you. It's about all of us and everything, and even now, while talking about this, his life is having an impact years later.

EXERCISE 43
Looking Back at The End

Imagine it is the end of your life on Earth and you have a chance to review everything you did on your unique journey.

Think about what your life contributed to?
Think about all that you accumulated?
How do the feelings differ?

Which makes you feel happier about the way you lived? The contribution you made or the possessions you had? Think about how your possessions are no longer yours but how your contribution lives on.

Imagine the people who helped you in your life, and those who maybe acted in ways you didn't see as help at the time, but which had a positive impact on your life indirectly?

Imagine all the people you helped and how their lives changed because of what you did or said?

Imagine the love you gave and how that radiated?

Imagine the shared laughter and how you enhanced the lives of those you met by being a beacon of lightness and love.

Imagine feeling grateful for the gift of life you were given and as you look back you can see the impact your life had on other life.

When we're aware of the impact our life has, that how we live affects other life and that our existence ripples on infinitely, it can transform how we live day to day and how we think, feel and act. We will be more focused on evolving and becoming more, and being the best gift we can to the universe, acting in a way which is the greatest thank you to that which created us. Be clear about your purpose and be happy, as that's the best version of you which you can share with everyone, whether your family, friends, work colleagues or strangers you interact with. It's also the greatest gift you can give yourself; lighting up the way you were designed to.

EXERCISE 44
Be a Beacon of Usefulment and Joy

For the next three days, focus on consciously being a beacon of usefulment and joy to everyone you come into contact with. Everyone from a shop assistant to your friends, family and work colleagues.

Think of yourself as a vessel whose purpose is to be of use to life around you.

Smile at strangers and be natural and warm and open – without being creepy!

Each evening informally review your thoughts:

How did that orientation make you feel?
How do you think it made others feel?
How do you think it changed the interactions you had?
Imagine the ripple effect of how you were with others and how they may then have been with people they interacted with.

Did you enjoy doing that and did you feel useful?

For some people, this may be a more dramatic change in approach than for others, but the purpose is to become more aware of the impact your orientation can have, and your own feelings. Of course, you cannot control how others react to you being such a beacon of usefulment and joy, but it would only be those who are not happy themselves who would be anything other than welcoming and warmed by such a giving orientation.

By having a clear, simple and easy to follow philosophy for the purpose of your life, you have a filter through which you can ask the same question of anything: "Does this fit with my purpose?" As this check becomes habitual, you'll feel life flowing naturally and you will love your journey, by enjoying yourself and knowing you're having a great impact on other life as you keep growing.

"The sole meaning of life is to serve humanity." – Leo Tolstoy

STEP 6
Appreciate Your Interconnectedness

"Learn how to see. Realise that everything is connected to everything else." – Leonardo da Vinci

There are more people alive today than ever before, and there are more and easier ways for everyone to connect because of advances in technology and transport. Most of us are also living closer to each other, yet people report themselves as feeling more apart. We are much less alone in the world yet we describe ourselves as being more lonely.

Both the UK and US governments have recently declared loneliness to be a big public health issue that affects all ages, not just older people living on their own. In the UK, a recent study described loneliness as an epidemic, claiming that 9 million people always or often feel lonely, and that a third of men admit to feeling lonely at least once a week. In a US study, nearly half of all American's described themselves as feeling lonely quite often. Some 54% said they feel like no one actually knows them well and approximately 40% said they lack companionship and feel isolated from others. More people are choosing to live alone, and more people see their life as apart from other people, even though it really isn't. Despite the growing population, the advancements in communication technology and the connective power of social media, the experience of loneliness seems to have never been more prevalent.

Say goodbye to loneliness

Seeing ourselves as separate is actually at the heart of most of our social problems. We are clearly less alone in the world than ever, but when we *think* we're more alone, we're programming ourselves to feel unhappy. If the world was a room, it's filling up, and the more people there are in the room, the more possibilities there are for interacting. You may not choose to interact, and you could be choosing to feel alone by how you think about the room and the people, but that's your decision.

This thing we call 'being lonely' usually tends to be described as something beyond our control and there is often an implication that loneliness is a problem the government should be sorting out. The SYSO System disagrees. Of course, we don't want people to feel lonely, but the responsibility lies with each of us, and implying it is anyone else's problem than our own to fix takes away the individual's responsibility and the power we have over how we experience our life. Loneliness-thinking is a form of victim-thinking and victim-thinking isn't going to help solve the issue in a sustainable way. Your thinking capacity could be put to a much more effective and enjoyable use.

In Stockholm, six in ten households have just one occupant, yet Swedes are less likely than the average European to complain of loneliness. 'Being' lonely can be more accurately described as 'doing' lonely and for most people, it is a choice. The solution is very simple; change how you think and you can stop 'doing' lonely thinking. Wake up to the important role you have in all life, the depth of your being, and the value you can add to other lives.

Loneliness and being lonely isn't something that is happening to us. We are actively doing lonely because of how we are thinking about ourselves and our role in the world. Loneliness is a pattern of thinking, and the way to start not feeling lonely, and to change the pattern, is to understand how important your contribution is to the whole. Understanding the interconnectedness of life and our role in this system changes the focus away from thinking about what we're getting from life, to how we can be a source of use and love to others, and when we do that we can spread good in the world rather than feeling sorry for ourselves by imagining that we're alone. We are never alone; there are more than 7 billion of us here!

The key to 'self-worth'

If someone is doing lonely by thinking they have low self-worth, which stops them choosing to interact with others, the best way to change that feeling would be for them to do something for others. They would then instantly feel they are being of use, and have worth. Your ultimate self-worth comes from your worth to life and this self-worth is pre-programmed; it is already within you.

If you feel lonely, then the first thing to do is reach out to connect with others in a giving way. Kindness, fun and compassion are always in demand, and if that's your focus you will never feel alone; you will feel useful and others will want to be with you. If you feel lonely, talk to someone, smile at them, compliment them, tell them how much they mean to you, write to them, send them a photo, make something for them, remind them how important they are to you, inquire about them, be interested, or remind them of a great memory of a time you shared. You don't need money to do any of this, you just need to be in a giving state of being. If you're miserable and complaining and telling people you're lonely, that isn't much fun for others and they'll only be with you out of sympathy, not because they like your company. Would you want people to be friends with you only because they feel sympathetic?

EXERCISE 45
BIG SOB

Anytime you think lonely thoughts, stop, look up at the sky and imagine fluffy white clouds in a clear blue sky forming the letters BIG SOB.

This isn't a self-pity, or invitation to cry prompt. This is your reminder; **B**e **I**n a **G**iving **S**tate **O**f **B**eing!

You can call on these reminder clouds at any time, and with practice this process will become a very healthy habit.

Before you know it, you won't even need the cue. You will have programmed yourself to be thinking more effectively and you will be more aware of your role as a valuable beacon in life.

You will naturally Be In a Giving State Of Being by default, and thoughts of being lonely will be obsolete programming.

Think of yourself as being a human aerial which receives signals but also gives signals. In the last chapter, we discussed how thinking of and acting as a transmitting beacon will lead to a much more fulfilling experience of life. If we focus on others and how we can be a ray of fun and usefulness in life, and how we can contribute to life, we'll feel much better about ourselves and people will want to be around us. Think of a social situation; do you prefer to spend your time around people who are givers or takers? We're not talking about giving in a material sense, although you can do that too, but more importantly in the giving of your spirit, your time, your kindness and your attention.

"We shall never know all the good a simple smile can do." – Mother Theresa

Our source is love

We exist because of others. We exist because of love from something other than ourselves. We exist because of the life energy we have within us which must have come from somewhere, it must have come from a source, and this source is always there. Every day we should be grateful to that which gave us life. Every day we should be grateful for our source which is always there. May the source be with you! This source is energy but it is also love, and that love which made us is always inside us. If you are struggling to feel this love that is always in you, focus instead on giving it. When you give love, you will feel love. The feeling is in you; love created you, and you are love. To feel your love, give your love. Yes, it really is as simple as that.

None of us exists in isolation. Even if you haven't seen anyone for a week, you live in a place that was likely built by others, you eat food that was made by others, you wear clothes designed and created by others, and you wash using plumbing supplies made by others. Think of your phone. How many times a day do you look at it? Your phone was designed and manufactured by others, has content created by others and it communicates on a network made and installed by others. The examples are endless but the bottom line is that no matter how you live your life, you depend on others far more than you likely realise.

We might physically be alone at times, but we always have a choice whether to think lonely thoughts or not. Of course, some people because of health or mobility limitations, find it very hard to even move, and they have less physical interaction because of this. Others are financially restricted, but with the internet and mobile phones, almost everyone can communicate with others and they can communicate to be a source of goodness to others. If you want more or better friendships, start with *giving* friendship or being a better friend. Give that which you want to receive is a fundamental principle of life.

EXERCISE 46
Pour Your Love and Kindness

For one week, pick a chunk of time each day when you have an opportunity to interact with others. It could be an hour or two depending on where you are and what you are doing. The exact length of time isn't important.

Decide for that period of time each day just to focus on how much love and kindness you can give. It could be giving in person, by letter, or with a phone call, but the idea is to focus as much as possible on giving the gifts of love and kindness.

Don't worry if you slip out of awareness now and again, just try and focus in every situation and interaction on pouring out love and kindness.

At the end of the week review how it felt:

Did it feel easy to be orientated that way?
Did others react to you differently?
Did it feel good?

You can do this exercise anytime. It is more of an ongoing conditioning regime than a specific exercise and making this orientation habitual and part of your identity will magnify the quality of your life experience.

If we feel lonely, we might need help with how we are thinking, and reprogramming the patterns of lonely thoughts. We are not passive victims who have somehow been unlucky enough to have been struck with the lonely stick, but we are actively doing lonely thinking whether that's consciously, or unconsciously. Not feeling lonely is a job for the individual, not others to do. Loneliness is simply a thinking pattern, or process, and we can stop doing it anytime we choose as long as we're aware of what is going on and when we know what to do.

All life is connected

We can choose to think about ourselves as a tiny, seemingly inconsequential grain in the whole scheme of life and because we are not physically attached to anyone or anything, we can think we're just on our own in a vast universe. Many people think like this, believing their life is finite and that they are separate from everything else. However, this type of programming and thinking about separateness and our life's end, isn't going to make us feel great. Instead, the key to appreciating the greater depth and expanse of our being lies in understanding that all life is connected. By appreciating the interconnectedness of everything we'll realise how the concept of loneliness is actually ridiculous.

When we change our thinking, we'll also be in the best position to reconnect others who feel disconnected by helping them tune into an appreciation of how everything is linked.

"You are never alone. You are eternally connected with everyone." – Amit Ray

Thinking about how you are interconnected with the world and having a clear philosophy for the important purpose of your life (Step 5) is the key to never feeling lonely. You are part of life and you don't just exist for yourself. You will be physically alone at times but you are never really alone in the world. Alone and lonely are very different. Being on your own isn't lonely and there are many examples of people who choose to spend much time without others being physically present. For men in the US, one of the most common fantasies is actually living in a log cabin in the wilderness. Buddhist monks choose to be alone for extraordinary amounts of time, yet they don't feel lonely. They experience regular solitude but they feel completely connected, as Buddhism at its core is based on the concept that everything is one. Ultimately, loneliness and unhappiness are usually the result of too much obsession with ourselves. Think about the unhappiest people you know. Do they run frequent self-pity thought patterns like 'poor me', 'it's so hard', 'life is unfair', and 'why me?' Now think about the happiest people you know and how they look at life differently. Would you describe them as lonely?

Before I get shot down and accused of being uncompassionate about loneliness, let's be clear. I am absolutely not questioning that we all have pain to deal with in various ways and at various stages of our life; one of our important human needs is to feel connection with others, and for some there is physical isolation on top of brutal physical illness. This book is about helping people help themselves and how everyone can make themselves feel better deliberately. How we choose to think about ourselves and in relation to others affects how we feel and therefore affects the quality of our life.

We are never cut off from life. Ever. Only if we choose to think and act in that way. We know from Step 2 that we can control how we think so we can control how we feel and act. When we're in the wilderness, we might be cut off from other humans but some who live, or have lived, alone in such an environment would claim they are even more connected to life, to all of nature and that they are definitely not lonely. Everything is connected. Everything, even if it may not feel so physically. If you crave other people to interact with, it's easier than it has ever been to connect. At this time in human evolution, there is no reason to not feel connected, especially as few of us live in the wilderness.

My mother, who is in her 80s, talks to a friend of a similar age regularly on the phone and says her friend often talks about feeling lonely. She complains that nobody has been to see her, no one has called or written for a while. My mother asked her, "Have you been out today?" No. "Have you called anyone?" No. "Have you written to anyone?" No. All those actions were possible for her but she chose instead to think of lonely being something she wasn't in control of, and in thinking like that she didn't take responsibility for how she wanted to feel. Friendship and connection are available to her and to everyone all the time, if we start by giving, or being the friend we would like others to be. Start with a BIG SOB.

"Never say you are alone, for you are not alone, your god and genius is within." – Epictetus

This chapter is about interconnectedness so you may wonder why it has started with so much about loneliness? By examining how our thinking determines feelings of loneliness, we can appreciate how being aware of our interconnectedness, and our role in life, can change how we are feeling and therefore how we behave. We are all interconnected. And how we think about our place in life is going to determine how we feel. We might feel inconsequential at times but as soon as we start becoming more aware that we're an integral part of something much bigger, we change our perspective on our living experience.

Instead of thinking how alone you are, think about how connected you are, how much life there is, how it has never been easier to connect with others, how there are more people than ever with all kinds of interests, and think about how you can contribute and be of use to others. There have never been more people and more ways to communicate with them, and wherever you are, whatever you're doing, it's because of other people. Nothing happens without help from others. We exist because of others, we are dependent on others and all life is interconnected with the past and the future in one inseparable web of life.

"To drop into being means to recognize your interconnectedness with all life, and with being itself. Your very nature is being part of large and larger spheres of wholeness." – Jon Kabat-Zinn

EXERCISE 47
Do Less Lonely

How lonely would you say you are?

Give yourself an intuitive loneliness score for your current life, out of 10. Don't overthink it, just give a number and write this down.

What percentage roughly of your life would you say you feel lonely to some degree? Again, write this down.

Now over the next few days commit to doing the following:

1. Talk to three new people each day. This can be anyone, a shop assistant, your bus or train driver, a neighbour. Ask them questions, it can be a short conversation, but it must be a conversation. Be interested in their answers and their life.

2. Smile at others. If you are used to keeping your head down or avoiding eye contact, this may seem a creepy exercise to you. Do it anyway; you'll probably benefit the most!

3. Give five compliments each day. Make them genuine and not sleazy. It could be as simple as saying something like: "Thank you, that service was fantastic, you're great," to waiting staff, or "I saw how kind you were to that person, it was really lovely" when you witness a kind act.

4. Each day contact someone you haven't heard from for a while. With all the technology available, this is easy. It could be a text message, an email or a call. Remind yourself to give friendship if you want to receive it.

5. Make a conscious decision to visit an elderly person or care home in the next ten days. Ask questions, listen, and help people polish some of their memories.

There are so many other things you could do, but do these five things as a start for a few days and then revisit your score. How lonely do you now feel on a scale of 1–10 and what percentage of your life do you feel lonely?

Everything exists to serve something more than itself

In looking at how everything in life is interconnected, let's start with thinking about the actual bodies that we live in. No part of our body exists in isolation or just for itself; it all has a purpose to serve something more than itself. This is a fundamental principle in life. Everything in life has a role to play, a purpose, an important part that is more than just itself. We all exist to serve something more than our self and all of life exists to support some other form of life.

The human body is made up of about 37 trillion cells and each on its own could easily seem completely inconsequential as such a tiny part of the whole, but they all work together and we only exist as a collection of all of them. They are all interdependent and if one of my cells is feeling lonely, it's likely just too focused on itself and its own importance rather than its purpose in the whole of my body! Think of any part of your body. The heart, for example doesn't exist just for the heart, the liver doesn't just exist for the liver. Every part of us has a role to play in a bigger part. Everything is connected and interdependent.

"Nothing is ever just in your head. Nothing is ever just in your body. They are intrinsically linked… always." – *Christiane Northrup*

EXERCISE 48
Become More Aware of How Your Body is Connected

Sit quietly and think of three different parts of your body.

These can be parts you can see or they can be internal parts which you know exist inside you.

Now for each part, think about what it does for other parts, and its importance to the overall system that is your body.

For example, if I think about my hand, it connects with my arm which helps me lift things such as putting food in my mouth. It senses when I touch things which sends a signal to my brain. It serves a purpose bigger than itself and it is interconnected with my whole body system.

If I think about my heart, it pumps blood to other parts of my body and I know my gut absorbs moisture from food, and processes waste amongst other things.

Whether my heart, liver, kidneys, eyes, feet or knees, each part of me has a purpose much bigger than itself. And if you go further into any part of your body, the parts are made up of smaller parts and these are all interconnected too.

Everything we are physically is interconnected, and this simple exercise, which we can do at any time, can help us tune into the interdependent system that is our body.

"The thing you realise when you get into studying neuroscience, even a little bit, is that everything is connected to everything else." – Paul Allen

In earlier exercises, you stepped into your personal life-viewing bubble and were able to float above your body, and back in time. You connected with earlier experiences and versions of yourself. Your past explains why you are where you are and has given you all the lessons you need for your life right now, preparing you to realise your future potential. Not everything will have gone the way you wanted but it was going the way you needed to be ready for the next part. We can't change the past but we can be grateful for the lessons and we absolutely can create the future we want based on the learnings and our vision and imagination. Our past, present and future are all connected.

EXERCISE 49
See How Life Affects Other Life

Jump into your life-viewing perspective bubble again and fasten up.

The journey of life started long before you were born, and it will continue long after you die. There may actually be no beginning and no ending to life, in the way humans think about these concepts.

When you are comfortable, float higher and higher above this moment until you can see your whole life journey laid out below.

Now imagine you can see very clearly your path so far, but you can also see this path stretching back and back infinitely before your time.

You can also see this path stretching out far ahead beyond today to an infinite future.

As you look down, imagine the section of path that is your life, lighting up. It becomes brightly illuminated with a warm golden glow and every aspect of your journey can be seen clearly. Feel grateful for the gift of every experience and every twist and turn.

Now, as you look back before your birth, the whole path before this starts to light up brightly too, and you can start to see the interconnectedness of everything that happened to make your life happen. You can see people who look separate, but the light shows you the way everything they did affected so much else, and that everyone and everything exists only because of everything before.

Travel back 100 years, 1000 years, 100,000 years to as far back as you can imagine and as you do, see the connections.

As you look down you can see the path leading from way back, to this moment, all illuminated with a golden glow and everything is so clearly visible.

Now imagine the path ahead starting to light up and revealing the impact of everything you do from now in your life, on everything in the future. You can see this path including friends, family, children, strangers you interact with, and you can see clearly how interconnected everything is, illuminated infinitely into the future.

When you are ready, float back down to the present moment and step out of your perspective bubble. Take some deep breaths, put your hand on your heart. Feel grateful for all life that has made your life possible, and commit now to being the most useful version of yourself to all future life.

Blaming the past

One of the common sources of unhelpful unhappy thinking is when we look at our life and wish things hadn't happened the way they did. We blame our past, we blame people, and we make excuses for how our life is now because of this. Everyone has crap that has happened, but what if it was supposed to play out the way it did? What if it was working for you, and for all life? No matter what has happened, be grateful for what your past has given you, what lessons you have learnt and have faith in the process and what lies ahead.

If you are going to blame your past, blame it effectively and make sure you acknowledge the positives that have come from it, even if much is yet unknown about why this needed to happen in your journey of growth. Let go and make peace with your past. It has passed and your job now is to take the learnings and focus on your impact on the rest of life. Don't carry crap with you. Crap is heavy and smelly and cumbersome! Instead put all the stuff you wished hadn't happened under your feet and use it as stepping stones to a higher place and an even more amazing future.

"Turn your wounds into wisdom." – Oprah Winfrey

EXERCISE 50
Blame Your Past Effectively

Think of something in your life that, when it happened, you thought it was terrible at the time. Perhaps a partner left you, you were betrayed or you lost a lot of money.

Now ask yourself what positive things have happened as a result of that 'bad' event.

Did a relationship break-up lead you to meet someone amazing you would not have otherwise met? Did it cause you to take a change of direction in your life? Who did you meet? What did you do that would not have otherwise happened?

If you were betrayed in business, what lesson did that give you, and what benefits have you reaped because of that?

If you are going to blame your past, make sure you also blame it for all the positive effects too, and be thankful for all the lessons you have learnt.

There is usually gold in what you think are your problems, and adversity can be your greatest teacher. As Rumi said – ***"The wound is where the light enters you.***

We are all perhaps closer to each other than we might think; you may have heard of the 'six degrees of separation' theory which suggests that every human on the planet is six or fewer social connections away from each other. In this sense, the world is smaller than we may imagine. If we start appreciating how we are all connected, all related and that everyone is just trying to do their best with what they have and where they are – even though their brain processing and programming has evolved differently – then we'll likely be more understanding and see more good in the world. Being interconnected is part of being human and we know from Step 4 that we all have the need to feel connection with others.

EXERCISE 51
The Chain of Events

Sit comfortably for a few moments and just let your thoughts flow, thinking about people who might have been involved in making the things around you. Your clothes, your furniture, your home, your car, and the food you are eating, for example.

Think of the chain of events that happened for each item. The number of people who would have been involved in design, development, production, distribution and selling.

Nothing is around you without a chain of prior events and people involved in those. Even if you made your own clothes or built your own house, you needed other people, and those people needed other people who needed others and so on.

As you think about this, you'll become more aware of the interconnectedness of everything and that will help you appreciate that the role we all have in life is never inconsequential.

"You cannot achieve success by yourself. It's hard to find a rich hermit." – Jim Rohn

EXERCISE 52
Make a Thank You List

Imagine standing at the end of your life and looking back.

Your life has completed and you are reviewing everything that has happened, in a similar way to Exercise 43.

What was most important to you in your life?

Was it the amount of money you accumulated, things you acquired, or your career?

Or was it the people in your life and what you did for others?

This time, make a list of people you would thank for the role they played in your life.

Just write down who you can remember, and see how the list quickly grows. Maybe one day you can write to some of those still alive, and tell them how much positive impact they had on your life.

We need others, and others need us in life.

"I needs we to be truly I." – Carl Jung

Life supports other life

All living things are connected to each other through the process that each organism depends on others for support. In order to thrive, plants get energy from the sun. We, as humans, receive the by-product from plants which is oxygen. Animals eat plants while other animals eat them, and on it goes in the food chain, with multiple branches being a great web of all life.

Life supports other life in some way even if we may not be aware of the processes going on in this incredible ecosystem. Bees, for example, pollinate the food supply and ants aid in decomposition by digging tunnels which aerates the soil and recycles nutrients. Termites consume decomposing plant matter, and bats provide night time insect control, saving crops and reducing the need for chemical pesticides. A single brown bat can eat up to 1000 mosquitoes in an hour. Frogs act as indicators of the health of their ecosystems as their permeable membrane can indicate contamination levels in both water and on land, and birds perform a broad variety of ecological roles including decomposition, pest control, nutrient recycling and seed dispersal. And spiders, one of the most feared animals, will consume most of the insects in your home.

In recent years, stocks of high-fat fish have been declining in the waters off the west coast of the US. This has caused the population of seals that eat the fish to decline. With fewer seals, the whales that normally feed on them have turned to eating sea otters. As the sea otters have diminished, the sea urchins they normally eat have increased in numbers, and because sea urchins like kelp, the kelp beds are now being decimated. There is more to this story but it's just an example of one simple ecosystem and the knock-on effects of a change in any part of the system.

Think of trees. They breathe in carbon dioxide and breathe out oxygen. Humans need to inhale oxygen and breathe out carbon dioxide. Trees and humans support each other's growth. Trees, like other green plants, use photosynthesis to convert the carbon dioxide into sugar, cellulose and carbohydrates that they use for food and growth. Trees also absorb other potentially harmful gasses, such as sulphur dioxide and carbon monoxide from the air and they release oxygen. One large tree can provide a day's supply of oxygen for four people. If we reduce the number of trees, we impact much more than just the trees.

"Here is a floating cloud in this sheet of paper. Without a cloud, there will be no rain; without the rain, the trees cannot grow; and without trees, we cannot make paper. If the cloud is not here, the sheet of paper cannot be here either." – Thich Nhat Hanh

Even a rock depends on its environment for its existence, needing specific temperatures and pressure so as not to melt or break down, and atoms depend on environmental conditions and the state of energy. Everything is connected to its environment since its existence depends on the conditions of the environment. The same life force is within all of us albeit in its own unique form, and every living expression has a role to play in the ecosystem. Life supports other life. Nothing exists on its own and even though we appear unconnected physically, we are interconnected in invisible ways in the whole system of life and through air, light, food and energy.

"There is a deep interconnectedness in all life on Earth, from the tiniest organisms, to the largest ecosystems, and absolutely between each person." – Bryant H. McGill

We are all distantly related

There is plenty of evidence to show that all of life's species are related and that we're all descended from a common ancestor. Charles Darwin reported evidence of these relationships over 150 years ago and he highlighted obvious anatomical similarities between both living and extinct diverse species. With his 1859 book *On the Origin of Species by Means of Natural Selection*, Darwin not only explained the diversity of life around us, but he also showed how all life is connected. More recent research has focused on showing how all organisms are related genetically and these relationships can be represented in an evolutionary tree known as the Tree of Life. We know now that most of what we consider to be resemblances are expressions of our shared genetic coding, which is the direct outcome of a common ancestry. If you have ever thought someone looks like a dog or a goat for example, you might be right, as it could well be a very real likeness because of this shared ancestry!

All life is made up of cells, and all cells in the human body except red blood cells contain chromosomes. These chromosomes are found in the nucleus of the cells and are made of DNA, which is a chemical called deoxyribonucleic acid, as well as protein. The DNA molecule has a double helix shape, which resembles a ladder twisted into a spiral shape, and its main purpose is to tell each cell what proteins it has to make which determines what the cell does. A gene is located in a chromosome and DNA is in these genes. It is DNA and genes which make each person individual, containing hereditary information about a person's genetic makeup and carrying all the information that is required to build and maintain an organism's cell. Scientists have been 'mapping' all genes on all human chromosomes in what has been called the Human Genome Project. It is estimated there are around 3 billion chemical base pairs that make up human DNA and approximately 20,000–25,000 genes. These genes define the way our body works, they affect the colour of our eyes, hair, skin etc. Half of every person's genes are acquired from each parent, which is why one child may resemble their mother, and the other their father.

There has been enormous research in this area and we're learning much more about how we are all individually biologically coded from a blend of genetic coding before us. There is still much to learn, but one thing is for sure; we're all distantly related. Darwin was the first person to lay out this idea and he showed his evidence that any two things share a common ancestor at some point in the past.

"Therefore, I should infer… that probably all the organic beings which have ever lived on this earth have descended from some one primordial form, into which life was first breathed." – Charles Darwin

The Tree of Life

The Tree of Life illustrates how different species arise from previous species via descent with modification, and that all of life is connected. We share a common ancestor with all primates, but we are also fish, in the sense that fish are the most recent common ancestors of all land animals. If you keep building back from this idea, eventually you reach the single common ancestor or last universal common ancestor (LUCA). Just about all evidence that researchers have been able to gather to date suggests that this universal common ancestor existed at some point between 3.5 and 3.8 billion years ago, and most scientists agree that it's a vastly more likely scenario that all life descended from a single ancestor than from multiple ones.

That we have evolved from other life, and we are interdependent on all life, are fundamental laws of nature. All forms of life survive by a mutual cooperation based on an innate recognition of their interconnectedness and often subtle interdependence. We are all part of – not apart from – everything, and many philosophers and spiritualists have long been aware the universe is a unified whole where all things are part of the system.

> *"Our relatedness with other living forms provides us something we solely need: a reverence for the life of all creatures great and small, and an expanded view of our place in nature – not as rulers over it, but as participants in it." – Larry Dossey*

Spirituality has often reached the same conclusions through intuition that philosophy has arrived at through reason, and which science has tried to prove through observation. Central texts of Hinduism, for example, talk of the unity of the mind. Buddhism is based on the principle that life manifests itself as oneness and the concept of *esho funi*, where *esho* is the environment, *sho* is life, and *funi* means inseparable.

Although we perceive things around us as separate from us, there is a primal level of existence in which there is no separation between ourselves and our environment, but a oneness. Separation is therefore an illusion and our inner life and exterior world are one and the same; we *are* what we have attracted in this world. Even Christianity, with its essentially dualist view of the cosmos with God as creator and the individual as the created, sees God as manifested on earth in the human form of Jesus Christ. God becomes man, the One becomes the individual and the many.

> *"Human mind has not woven the web of life. We are but one thread within it. Whatever we do for the web, we do to ourselves. All things are bound together. All things connect." – Chief Seattle*

We are part of the unity of all being. Everything depends on something else for its existence and therefore all existence is relational. Life is connected because it comes from the same LUCA and information with function is passed on and modified over time. It is all one force with each bit interacting with other bits. The tree of life, although made up of many branches, is still only one tree.

Everything is a self-supporting ecosystem and is part of something bigger. We can only try and analyse the concepts of bigger and bigger and smaller and smaller within the limitations of our human processing. Maybe there is no maximum big and no minimum small, or no beginning and no end, and these are just human ideas?

The cosmic web

Some people think that the universe is just a hodgepodge of various planets, stars and galaxies. But over the years, scientists have found evidence that the universe may not be random, and rather it is actually more organised and interconnected than we could have ever imagined.

Earth is part of a solar system, and our solar system is one of many planetary systems and stars that make up the Milky Way Galaxy. The Milky Way Galaxy as well as thousands of other galaxies, such as the Andromeda Galaxy, belong to a collection of galaxies called the Local Galactic Group. The Local Galactic Group is part of the Virgo Supercluster of galaxies, which some scientists say is one of about 10 million such galactic superclusters. Struggling to understand the scale of this? Me too, but let's just say that's a lot of planets, solar systems, galaxies and superclusters and all of these superclusters and everything we think we know in the universe forms an immense network called the cosmic web.

So, what do we know about these planets and this web? Firstly, all planets are in constant motion and, like the human body, they all resonate, circulate heat, and move around a central sun. Like humans, the solar system produces energy, it circulates heat and moves around a galaxy. Just like you, the galaxy resonates, it circulates heat, and it moves around a central universal core. Every human being, each planet, every sun and star, and each galaxy travels at its own pace and on its own track. Everything in this vast universe is in its own little world, yet we are all connected moving together in a fine-tuned and very precise symphony. The next time you feel isolated, or inferior or superior to any other form of life, think about this connection. Humans are but a small piece of a massive creation. Changes in the universe affect our galaxy. Changes in our galaxy effect our solar system. Changes in our solar system affect the Earth. And changes on our planet affect human beings.

The universe is expanding and it seems likely it started from something very small, even though we can't explain what started this and why. It is expanding from a common point or singularity and astronomers can see that galaxies are moving away from us at speeds proportionate to their distance. This is called Hubble's law, after Edwin Hubble who made this discovery in 1929. It suggests that the universe was once compacted. The physicist Stephen Hawking believed if we wound back to the start of the universe, the starting point was a single atom, but even he is unable to provide a theory for what happened before this

> *"Events before the big bang are simply not defined, because there's no way one could measure what happened at them. Since events before the big bang have no observational consequences, one may as well cut them out of the theory and say that time began at the big bang." – Stephen Hawking*

There are some things which we just can't understand in our lifetime, but it does seem likely that if we rewind time, we go back to a single something, whatever we choose to call it, and everything is expanding from that. We are all derived from the same source, we all related to this source, and this source of all life is always in all of us, like a ray from the sun is always from the sun. We are interconnected in terms of our make-up and origin, and our present is all connected with our past, and the future is connected to the present. We are also connected to all other forms of life and everything in the universe is like a three-dimensional interconnection or giant ball of infinite, hard-to-comprehend connections.

EXERCISE 53
Building Awareness That Everything is Interconnected

Sit calmly, close your eyes and take several deep breaths.

Focus on your body, being aware of the different parts.

Start with your feet and work up, thinking about how the parts of your body are interconnected.

When you are ready, think about your life and how it is connected to your past. Where you are right now is because of all the events that happened before, as you saw with the illuminated path of all time in Exercise 49.

Think about the future and how what you do next links to everything in your future.

Next, think about other people and how you are connected, starting with those closest to you.

Think of all forms of life, animals and plants, and all of nature as one big ecosystem of which you are interconnected and interdependent.

Think of this ecosystem as part of a bigger ecosystem, which in turn is part of something bigger.

Think of the universe and everything at the highest level you can.

It is all interconnected.

We are one

As everything is interconnected, nothing exists in isolation. We are a part of life, and everything affects other life. If you can open your mind to the unity that is the universe, you can begin to transcend your mental programming and awaken to the deeper reality that we are not simply here as recipients of life, but we are shapers and creators participating in the universe. We are one. We might feel divided by borders, religions, politics or cultural programming but these concepts are all self-created in our minds.

We are all part of the expansion of life, but we are also part of the past, the present and the future. We are all one. We know we are connected by what we can see but we are also connected by invisible forces of interconnection such as electromagnetic fields and energy waves (Step 7) and likely other invisible forces we are not aware of. Even our thoughts don't exist in isolation; they too are all interconnected as nothing exists solely on its own.

From the tiniest atomic particle to the biggest galaxies, the past, the present and the future of every animate and inanimate being is defined by its interconnection to everything else. Western culture discourages us from realising we are all one, but when we wake up and become aware that we are all interconnected and interrelated in a oneness, we can dramatically change our experience of life and the relationships we have with other parts of our universe.

Culturally we are programmed to believe that we are autonomous individuals, isolated from the world around us by the boundaries of our bodies. However, we are interdependent organisms connected to both living organisms and non-living natural objects. Like the rocks, mountains, lions and ants, we are all made from the same basic atomic materials. We are equal partners with everything else in the universe but the greatest obstacle to ecological sustainability on Earth is a worldview that places humanity as separate from and superior to the rest of nature. Everything in nature is interconnected and life on Earth would cease to function if interconnectivity did not exist.

"A human being is a part of the whole, called by us 'Universe', a part limited in time and space. He experiences himself, his thoughts and feelings as something separate from the rest—a kind of optical delusion of his consciousness. The striving to free oneself from this delusion is the

one issue of true religion. Not to nourish it but to try to overcome it is the way to reach the attainable measure of peace of mind." – Albert Einstein

All of nature's patterns are also manifestations of interconnected, interdependent networks of conduits that transform and transport our sun's energy to everything on our planet. Without these networks of energy flow, all objects and creatures on Earth would cease to exist. Each energy network interacts with energy conduits in larger and smaller networks. A human being, a tree, a mountain stream, a maturing ecosystem and the Earth's evolving biosphere are all interconnected dynamic networks that direct energy flow in nature. A river and a human being don't look anything like each other, but their energy transportation networks do, and they perform similar functions. Think of a tree. The twigs in a tree support leaves that capture the sun's energy. The green chlorophyll in a leaf's energy transforms and stores that captured energy. Some of that energy is transported to the rest of the tree through twigs, branches and trunks. Twigs are connected to branches in similar ways. Branches are connected to trunks in much the same way. Each branch or twig in the tree's structural hierarchy is a magnified or reduced version of its immediate neighbor in a phenomenon called 'self-similarity' because each structure looks similar to other structures in the tree. The structures are called 'fractals' and it has been shown that many different energy transportation and transformation systems in nature are fractal. A tree's root system captures nutrients and other energy forms from the earth. Roots look much like fractal collections of twigs and branches. These roots intertwine with root systems from other trees as well as various subterranean ecosystems.

Our lungs and our blood transportation systems are fractal structures that interrelate with each other. Our systems of nerves are fractal. River systems are fractal. Indeed, much of the energy in nature is transported and transformed by networks that have the same fractal structure that we see in trees. Looking at these interconnected 'self-similar' systems of energy flow gives us a sense that some kind of unity exists and there is growing scientific proof that the way all living creatures process energy is similar. Science is now beginning to show what the spiritual and aesthetic worldviews have known for a long time; that nature does have a common thread and that we are all connected.

"Everything is interrelated. The universe must be viewed as one, as a whole. We are all one. We are all part of the same whole." – Rav Berg

What ripples are you creating?

Having an appreciation of this interdependence helps us understand the greater importance of everything we do. Everything has an impact far beyond itself. Every action, and every communication causes a ripple of effect, even though the effects are mostly invisible to us. Think of everything you do in the world, every interaction, and think whether you are causing a positive ripple or triggering a negative chain of events. Never underestimate the impact of anything you do as it can extend infinitely even though we are unaware of the path it takes. An act is like an energy; it has to go somewhere so it will keep going or change into some other form of energy.

If you give someone a compliment or do something kind, that person will probably feel good about that and they are more likely to interact with others in a positive way as a result. Imagine driving and someone has been waiting to pull onto the road you are on, but so far, no other drivers have let them out. Imagine that you slow down and wave them to go. They pull out and wave back. You might feel good for a moment and then forget about what just happened but that small act, like every act, has consequences and is a trigger for what happens after. What if your kind act made the other driver feel good and reminded them that there was kindness in the world? What if they were on their way to work where their colleague is then impacted by their kindness and upbeat feelings, and what if the colleague is a research assistant at a hospital or university and their lifted spirits causes them to interact differently with another colleague who is working on a cure for cancer? What if that interaction changed something in her actions that led to her trying something different that led to a great scientific breakthrough that saved thousands of lives?

This is of course an exaggerated imaginary scenario, but the point is that we never know the extent of the impact we have on the world with the smallest of our acts, our words and our attitudes. When you think of yourself as a beacon transmitting into the universe, you step into the power of your being, and you can become more aware of how everything you do never stops with just the moment of doing. Be positive, kind and loving and you are sending positivity, kindness and love out into the universe. Moreover, we know the universe is all one so you're actually sending this not just to everything in the universe but also back to yourself.

And of course, the opposite is true. When you do or say something negative, selfish or inconsiderate, the impact goes beyond what you did. Imagine you said something sharp, unreasonable and hurtful to a waiter serving you in a restaurant. That the waiter then goes back to the kitchen in a foul mood and starts berating the chef, who starts doing frustrated and angry thinking which affects how he feels. He storms out of the restaurant as soon as his shift is finished and goes to the train station where he is rude and aggressive to the train ticket inspector. The train inspector is about to leave to walk home to babysit his grandchildren but he is flustered and running late and arrives in a bad mood, which causes tension with his daughter as he is late and then the children wake and one falls trying to come downstairs. Again, this is a very extreme example but it encourages our awareness that there is a never-ending impact of everything we do and say; even one small act somewhere can have enormous consequences somewhere else. The ripple effect goes on and on infinitely and our actions really do change the world. The question to ask ourselves isn't, will I make a difference in the world – the real question is, what kind of difference will it be?

"We cannot live for ourselves alone. Our lives are connected by a thousand invisible threads, and along these sympathetic fibres, our actions run as causes and return to us as results." – Herman Melville

Being a great human means consciously trying to magnify the positive ripples you cause and diffusing or minimising the negative ripples. Being kind and happy and giving is the greatest benefit you can give to life. Be a beacon of joy, kindness and love and you will see the change in how people interact with you. It really all starts with love. What we are describing is active rippling, but there is also a lot of invisible stuff we're unaware of. Our energy field and our vibrations, our thoughts and other invisible pathways of our presence and mood are all transmitting from us as a force impacting and rippling way beyond ourselves. It is a gift to the world to be in a good mood, radiating out good vibrations, and it is a pain to the world to be grumpy or in a negative vibrational state. Whatever vibration you give keeps on giving. You can be a diffuser of ripples of negativity, being the one to turn it around.

Start with understanding, not judging, and start with love not fear. When we pause and see how interconnected we are, we'll realise it's impossible to not have an effect on others far beyond our knowing. We will never know the full effect our life has on other lives.

Interdependence

Nothing we ever do stops. Every act is a link in an endless chain that is connected with all the other links. And this chain of the universe unites all objects and processes in a single whole. Even by moving our finger we 'disturb' the whole universe which is an infinite web of connections, which interact either through various fields or by means of direct contact. In a crystal for example, which is a mix of atoms, no individual atom can move in complete independence of the others. Its slightest shift has an effect on every other atom.

If we become more aware of the interdependence of everything then our respect for every other living thing in the universe will change. Realising we are all one, that we are all in this together and we are all on the same team will make us more sensitive to the consequences of all our actions and lead to a happier, more peaceful and loving life.

"Meditate often on the interconnectedness and mutual interdependence of all things in the universe." – Marcus Aurelius

Thinking of being separate is at the heart of many of our problems. We must awaken from this illusion of separateness, and become more aware of what Larry Dossey calls our 'expansive consciousness', embracing the whole of nature in a 'nonlocal mind'. Even though we may live our lives in our local minds and ordinary reality, we are unconscious participants in this larger nonlocal mind. By being happy, loving and grateful you are giving the greatest gift you can to this larger consciousness and you are being most aligned with your purpose of enjoying life and helping others.

"The idea that everything is purposeful really changes the way you live. To think that everything you do has a ripple effect. That every word that you speak, every action that you make affects other people and the planet." – Victoria Moran

STEP 7
Raise Your Vibration

"If you want to find the secrets of the universe, think in terms of energy, frequency and vibration." – *Nikola Tesla*

Everything in our universe is interconnected and moving, because of the force we call energy. Let's start with you. Try and sit absolutely still for a moment. When you're sitting as still as you think you possibly can, ask yourself; is anything moving? Whether you're aware of it or not, your body is always moving. It is a system of systems, of organs and cells which are always active, growing, transforming and replenishing. Our bodies are always in a state of movement even if we think we're still, and our organs are processing 24/7, whether our heart, liver, kidneys or lungs.

We inhale around 1000 times per hour and with each breath, our lungs expand and contract as the air is processed. When we breathe in, the diaphragm contracts and moves downward, increasing the space in our chest cavity. Our lungs then expand and the muscles between our ribs move to enlarge the chest cavity, pulling the ribcage upward and outward before you exhale in a process that allows the exchanging of oxygen from the environment for carbon dioxide from the body's cells. Just in relation to your breathing, processing and movement is happening all the time.

Even if you held your breath to try and briefly be still, your heart will be beating around 4000 times an hour, without you having to consciously do anything. It is continuously pumping oxygen and nutrient-rich blood throughout your body to sustain life, expanding and contracting about 100,000 times per day, pumping six or seven litres of blood every minute. Your blood is the river of life, and it's constantly moving huge volumes of liquid inside you, through a complex system of veins and arteries.

Think about your eyes. Not only are they moving as you process things you see, and as your brain does its thinking, but your eyelids close and open on average every four seconds, or around 900 times an hour, with each blink lasting about 1/10th of a second. Every time you blink, your eyelids spread oils and mucous across the surface of your eyes to keep them from drying out. Even when you're asleep, your eyes are moving, with the brain usually working through five different stages of sleep including rapid eye movement (REM) where the eyes move rapidly in various directions.

You are always moving

You can never be absolutely still. Your world within is always moving. The estimated 37 trillion cells that make up our bodies are always moving, changing, renewing, constantly communicating with each other and keeping our heart beating, digesting our food, eliminating toxins, protecting us from infection and disease, and generally being very busy carrying out all the functions that are keeping us alive. Even on the outside of our body, on the surface of human skin, scientists believe there are over 150 species of bacteria which are in constant motion. Our hair and nails are growing, we sweat, and we discharge processed waste in various ways. We get bigger or smaller, always being in a state of change.

> *"Nothing is static. Energetic frequencies are changing all the time. We, and everything in our world, are made of energy and as such, we too are changing… with or without our awareness."* – *Elaine Seller*

Our brain constantly impulses, with neurons firing and chemicals being released. Even if you try and quieten your mind and not really think of anything, electrical and chemical processes are still happening. Thinking is the nature of your brain. It is always doing thinking, even if you slow the processes; you simply can't stop thinking. You can focus and channel your thoughts effectively, you can detach from the thoughts you have and become a witness and observer of them rather than reacting, but you can't stop the *process* of thinking. If you are meditating, being mindful or even sleeping, your brain is still very active. To think, dream, imagine or rest is all activating your brain chemistry. Your brain is stimulated and converts brain sparks into chemicals which swim around and cause the energetic reactions in your body to create your feelings.

Your body may appear to be a solid structure, but it's actually really a process, a constant flow of energy and information changing all the time. Your body right now is not exactly the same body you had earlier today as the cells are constantly changing and talking to each other. Your body is basically a giant nonstop production, processing, communication, transport and waste disposal system, working 24/7 every day of your life and your unconscious mind is managing all of this.

Our bodies are movement, and movement is a key to keeping them healthy. We are born as moving creations, with energy flowing through what is a miracle system. It is physically impossible to be still and it really doesn't make much sense if we tell for example, our children to sit still.

"Movement is life. Life is a process. Improve the quality of the process and you improve the quality of life itself." – Moshe Feldenkrais

Our body system is in a constant state of communication within itself and it has its own built-in intelligence that is always there whether we're aware of this or not. Your heart, which was being created before you had a brain, may be the core of your innate intelligence system. Scientists have been researching how the heart thinks for itself and communicates with the brain, or in many ways can be considered a brain itself. Perhaps all parts of your body think for themselves. We know everything in life is interconnected and everything is a system, and so communication within our body must be happening in this same interconnected way, whether we're aware of this or not.

EXERCISE 54
Appreciate the Processes That Are Your Body

Sit calmly and take several slow deep breaths. With each inhale and exhale, think about the flow of air into your lungs, with fresh oxygen being distributed into your blood and to your cells, and these cells then disposing of their waste which is exhaled by your lungs and pushed out through your mouth.

Become aware of just how much there is to the process of taking a single breath, and how there is continual movement with this simple act of breathing.

Next, think about your heart. Feel it beating. Imagine with each beat, the journey of your blood being pumped which is giving life and nutrition to your cells, travelling along arteries and veins.

Think about food. You take it in your mouth, then you chew and swallow and it passes down your throat and into your stomach. Think about the entire process of digestion and the journey of the food with some elements being absorbed and some passing out of you as waste.

Now bring awareness to other parts of your body and imagine the processes when you blink, when you look at something, when you hear a sound.

Of course, you can do this exercise for any of your body processes, at any time and wherever you are. And by bringing occasional consciousness to what's going on inside, you will also be building your appreciation for the miracle system that you are.

Humans are always in motion. Our bodies are always doing processes, and constant movement is the same for all forms of life whether they are other closely related animals, or insects, or even plants and trees. Life equals movement and movement is a result of energy. Life in any form is energy, and not only is everything inside all forms of life moving, so is everything outside.

EXERCISE 55
Become Aware That Everything is Moving

Look around you wherever you are. What can you see that is moving?

Look up if you are outside – are there clouds, and if so, are they moving?

Can you see or hear birds moving?

Is there a breeze? Is rain falling, are insects flying, are any trees moving or leaves blowing?

There will almost certainly be noises and changes in the environment wherever you are.

Build your awareness and consciousness of the movement that is life, all around you at any time.

Everything is moving, wherever you are.

The movement of air

Think of the air. Even if you are in a quiet dark room, molecules in the air are moving around you in many directions and at about 1000 miles per hour, colliding with dust particles. Just like everything else in the universe, this air is made up of atoms and molecules. Scientists have for a long time been trying to bring atomic-sized particles to a 'still' position but they've not succeeded, and all research supports the theory that absolutely nothing in our universe is totally still. The universe is a system of moving energy.

The air in which we all exist is an invisible mix of gases, mostly nitrogen (78%), oxygen (21%), and carbon dioxide (0.3%). Movement of these gases is caused by temperature or pressure differences, which are experienced as wind when we're outside. Where there are differences in pressure between two places, a pressure gradient exists, and air moves from the high-pressure region to the low-pressure region following a spiralling route; outwards from high pressure and inwards towards low pressure. This spiralling is caused by the rotation of the Earth beneath the moving air, which causes an apparent deflection of the wind to the right in the Northern Hemisphere, and to the left in the Southern Hemisphere caused by what scientists call the Coriolis force.

Waves of energy

Many things are moving which are not visible to us and which we are unlikely to be aware of. We may be conscious of movement in the form of waves such as sound, light and Wi-Fi, even if we don't really understand 'how' they operate. There are many waves in the electromagnetic spectrum, such as radio, microwaves, infrared, ultraviolet, x-rays and gamma rays which are moving all around us. Each wave is a wave of energy but each has its own individual properties and is in some way different from every other wave. Life, it seems, is essentially differences and movement.

"Genius is finding the invisible link between things." – Vladimir Nabokov

Soundwaves carry noises through the air to our ears. Seismic waves travel inside the Earth and cause earthquakes. Light, heat and radio energy are all carried by a variety of waves in the electromagnetic spectrum. Some energy waves need a medium through which to travel and the medium itself moves back and forth as the waves carry energy through it. When an ocean wave, for example, crashes against the shore, it releases a large amount of energy but waves also carry huge amounts of energy across the surface of the sea as they travel and move. A wave three metres high carries enough energy to power around 1000 lightbulbs in every metre of its length.

All existence can actually be explained by wave properties, and the flow and patterns of energy. We have waves of energy that are moving inside us constantly, including thought waves and the waves of emotion. All these waves, whatever type they are, have a structure and properties such as frequency, period, amplitude, wavelength and speed. If we are going to manage our internal worlds more effectively, it is useful to understand at least a little about the properties of frequency and amplitude.

> *"We are slowed down sound and light waves, a walking bundle of frequencies tuned into the cosmos. We are souls dressed up in sacred biochemical garments and our bodies are the instruments through which our souls play their music." – Albert Einstein*

Frequency is the number of wave cycles that are completed in one second, measured in hertz (Hz), named after Heinrich Rudolf Hertz, and so a wave with a frequency of 20 Hz completes 20 wave cycles every second. If a frequency is vibrating fast enough, it's emitted as a sound and if it vibrates faster, it's emitted as a colour of light. Each category of waves has a frequency spectrum. In the spectrum for visible light, violet is at the top with the highest frequency. At the bottom is red, which has the lowest frequency, and if waves have frequencies lower than red or higher than violet, it's not possible for humans to see them.

The amplitude of a wave is measured by its height and how much energy is being transported by the particular wave. The greater the amplitude (more height), the more energy a wave has and the lower the amplitude (less height), the less energy is transported. Our thoughts and the emotional energy they cause to move in different ways around our bodies, are waves in exactly the same way as other waves and so they too have different frequency and amplitudes.

Your energy vibrates and this vibration produces waves flowing inside you, but these waves also flow out from you. You are a beacon, transmitting invisible waves of your energy out into the world. If your thoughts are negative, you'll emit waves with low frequencies and amplitudes and if your thoughts are positive, you'll emit waves with high frequencies and amplitudes. By managing your mind more effectively (Step 2) and taking charge of your emotional energy (Step 3), you can focus on ensuring your thought patterns are creating waves with high frequencies and amplitude, by positive happy empowered thinking. This will not only make you feel great because of your higher vibration, but you'll also be transmitting more positivity to others.

"Your energy introduces you even before you speak." – Anon

Understanding your brainwaves

Scientists are understanding more about how energy flows, as machines for measuring electric impulses are becoming more sophisticated. It is now commonly accepted that neurons in our brains fire together in rhythmic patterns like a kind of clapping, and the frequency of these patterns is measured like all waves; in hertz or cycles per second. Slow clapping, or slow waves, therefore measure as low frequency and fast clapping or fast waves measure as high frequency. Modern equipment for measuring brain electrics shows that there are five basic brainwave types in terms of frequency; delta, theta, alpha, beta and gamma. Understanding these five types of brainwaves can help our self-management, and learning about how we can best use of each of these brain states. They all have a frequency range and each wave type controls a variety of states of consciousness ranging from sleep to active thinking. While all brainwaves work simultaneously, one brainwave can be more dominant and active than the others and the dominant brainwave will determine our current state of mind.

Delta brainwaves are slow, less than 4Hz. They tend to be generated in deepest meditation and dreamless sleep, and when delta brainwaves are dominant, external awareness is suspended. It is believed that healing and regeneration are stimulated in this state, and this is why deep restorative sleep is so essential to the healing process.

Theta brainwaves, with a frequency of around 4–8Hz, occur most often in REM sleep but are also dominant in meditation and believed to be a gateway to learning, memory and intuition. In theta, our senses are withdrawn from the external world and focused on signals originating from within, and it is a state which we normally only experience briefly as we wake or drift off to sleep. In theta, we are in a dream with vivid imagery, intuition and information beyond our normal conscious awareness and where we hold many of our unconscious fears.

Alpha brainwaves (8–12Hz) are dominant during quietly flowing thoughts and in some meditative states, being described by some as waves of being here in the present moment. Alpha is a resting state for the brain and it is believed these waves aid our overall calmness, alertness, learning and our mind–body integration.

Beta brainwaves (12–40Hz) dominate our normal waking state of consciousness when attention is directed towards cognitive tasks and the outside world. Beta is a 'fast' activity, present when we are alert, attentive, engaged in problem-solving, judgement, decision-making, or focused mental activity. Beta waves are often described as low or high, where low is a calm, focused mental state and high could be when you are anxious or stressed. In high beta, the waves shut down brain regions that handle rational thinking, decision-making, memory and objective evaluation. Blood flow to the 'thinking brain' can be reduced by as much as 80%. Being starved of oxygen and nutrients, our brains ability to think then clearly plummets.

Gamma brainwaves (greater than 40Hz) are the highest frequency or fastest waves and they relate to simultaneous processing of information. They are associated with high levels of intellectual function, creativity, peak states or what we might call feeling 'in the zone.' Scientists believe they flow from the front to the back of the brain about 40–100 times per second. Researchers have also more recently discovered that gamma waves are highly active when in states of love and altruism and it's speculated that a greater presence of gamma rhythms relates to expanded consciousness and spiritual emergence.

Our brainwaves are like musical notes making a symphony. The higher and lower frequencies all interconnect with each other and the waves change according to what we are doing and feeling. When slower brainwaves are dominant, we can feel tired, sluggish or dreamy and when the higher frequencies are dominant, we likely feel wired, or hyperalert. Our brainwave profile and our daily experience of the world is constantly changing and when the waves are out of balance, research has identified patterns associated with various mental conditions. Over-arousal in certain brain areas is linked with anxiety disorders, sleep problems, impulsive behaviour, anger and aggression. Under-arousal in certain areas is believed to lead to some types of clinical depression and insomnia. By becoming more aware of the different brainwave states we're experiencing and by learning how to proactively effect different states, we will be taking charge and can use our minds better to work for us, rather than reacting to wave patterns unconsciously.

Our brains activate and constantly transmit waves, but they also receive waves. Thoughts, ideas, information and knowledge from the universe can be tapped into depending on the habitual frequency of your own thoughts and emotions. It all starts with energy and frequency. Everything is interconnected, and you can be a better manager of what you transmit and receive when you understand and better manage your frequencies.

Energy waves have long been the focus of studies. Guglielmo Marconi, the Italian inventor, showed the world the feasibility of radio communication and that signals could be sent without wires. He sent and received his first radio signal in Italy in 1895 and a wireless signal from Newfoundland to Ireland a little later. Nikola Tesla also worked in this area and proved similar ideas, mathematically and physically. However, even though scientists have been studying invisible waves for a long time, it's only the more commonly used and commercial applications which we're likely to be most aware of.

Beyond our senses

Think about the remote control for your TV. At the end of the unit, there's a small light emitting diode (LED) where infrared radiation comes out, and on the TV is a very small infrared light detector. When you press a button, a beam of infrared radiation travels from the remote to your TV at the speed of light and the detector picks it up. Human eyes can't detect these infrared remote-control waves, but some animals can. We describe these waves as invisible but they should more accurately be described as 'invisible to humans'.

Rattlesnakes, for example, can detect infrared waves as they have detectors near their eyes, which work like the infrared detectors on the TV, and by homing in on infrared heat, snakes can locate prey in the dark. Some animals, such as eagles, hedgehogs and shrimp, can see into the lower reaches of the ultraviolet spectrum.

Humans have invented radar guns, magnetic compasses and infrared detectors to stretch beyond the limits of our five natural senses, but many animals already have these capabilities built in. There are also many more sensory capabilities outside those which humans are gifted with. Understanding these limitations and that we can only experience life through a limited range of senses, might help us appreciate and be humble that there is a lot more to the universe than we can likely ever know in this existence.

Think of the incredible sense of hearing which we have. Dolphins, bats and some shrews, however, have a much greater hearing capacity and they use echolocation to navigate their surroundings. They emit high-frequency soundwaves or pulses, that are either very high-pitched to human ears or completely inaudible, and then detect the echoes produced by those sounds. Special ear and brain adaptations enable these animals to build three-dimensional pictures of their surroundings in the way doctors use echo scanning tools for imaging tests like pregnancy and heart scans.

Electric fields produced by some animals also function like senses. Electric eels for example, and some species of rays, have special muscle cells that produce electric charges strong enough to shock and sometimes kill their prey. Other fish use weaker electric fields to help them navigate murky waters and find prey. Sharks possess the best biological conductor of electricity yet discovered, as they have a jelly that fills a network of pores all around their face. As they swim towards prey the jelly detects the smallest of differences between the electrical charge of the animal and the water around it, like a homing device that guides the shark to its feed even in the darkest water.

Mantis shrimp are famous for striking prey so hard that the water around them gets very hot. Light polarisation can rotate clockwise or counter-clockwise, giving what's called a circular polarisation and mantis shrimp notice patterns in this that are invisible to every other animal on Earth. To facilitate signalling and mating, their eyes have evolved filters that can distinguish between the two circular polarisations.

The movement of molten material in the Earth's core and the flow of ions in the Earth's atmosphere generate a magnetic field that surrounds the planet. Just as compasses point toward magnetic north, animals possessing a magnetic sense can orient themselves in specific directions and navigate long distances. Animals as diverse as bees, sharks, sea turtles, rays, migratory birds and salmon all have magnetic senses. How these animals actually sense Earth's magnetic field is not yet known but it could be due to small deposits of magnetite in their nervous systems acting like microscopic compass needles. Even the lowly worm relies on a single nerve that detects Earth's magnetic field and orients them accordingly so they aren't upside down.

Bees use the hair on their legs to detect a flower's electromagnetic field and although they rely on many variables to find roses in your garden, one of the most important is voltage. They accumulate a small positive charge as they fly, and flowers have a negative charge. The hairs on their legs respond to the attraction between these opposite charges, guiding them to flowers, and this charge changes once a bee stops, so other bees know to move along.

Vampire bats can sniff out veins using special proteins which tell them when they are above warm skin, and where there is likely to be a juicy blood vessel hiding underneath. The butterfly has at least 15 different types of photoreceptors in its eyes and it has hairs on its wings to detect changes in air pressure, and elephants communicate in all sorts of ways as they trumpet and flap their ears and rumble at frequencies so low you might feel it, but never hear it. Their feet and trunks are sensitive enough to pick up vibrations created by other elephants as far as ten miles away and even more amazingly, they can tell if the stomper is a friend or a stranger, and use subtle differences in what each foot feels to understand the source.

Many animals have a much stronger sense of smell than humans. Dogs, for example, have about 600,000 olfactory neurons in a specialised recess, which is about 15 times the amount humans have, and which is why dogs are great for use in drugs sniffing and finding skiers in avalanches and mountain rescue. Not only do dogs have powerful, super-sensitive smell capabilities, they have much more sensitive hearing than humans, hearing sounds four times farther away and picking up much higher frequency sounds than we can.

The examples above show just a small selection of animals with sensory capabilities different to humans, and it is without doubt that we have, in relative terms, a very limited sensory capacity. It's therefore important to stay humble and curious about life rather than ever thinking we know everything, or that we are superior as humans. We share the planet with creatures that can smell veins, see colours we can't imagine, hear sounds we don't hear and who can communicate through their feet. All of this is because of energy, and energy moving in different waves. We know there are many types of these waves, but the key point to take is to be acutely aware that energy is causing movement everywhere and in everything. Everything is energy.

Our electromagnetic field

Scientists today have equipment which can test for the electric charges humans are transmitting. Our body is constantly processing and the electricity we are generating from all of our body workings, not just our brains, creates an electromagnetic field which can actually be measured. We have a powerful overall electromagnetic field, extending about 15 feet from our physical bodies, and different parts of us have their own individual energy fields such as the lungs, the brain and the heart, with all parts being in systems that are part of larger systems inside us.

The heart has an electromagnetic field believed to be 40–60 times stronger than the brain's, and there is an increasing amount of study looking at how important it is for our heart to be aligned electrically with our brain and all our body systems. The leader in the field of research in this area is the HeartMath Institute, which we already mentioned in Step 3. They have conducted extensive studies that show we will feel most at peace and content in our life when our heart energy is aligned with our brain energy in a state of coherence. The HeartMath Institute's understanding is that through an unseen electromagnetic energy emitted by the heart, humans are profoundly connected to all living things, and that it is the energy of our hearts that literally links us to each other. We are all part of and contribute to the collective energy field. The HeartMath Institute has already conducted extensive research on the power of the heart, the heart–brain connection, heart intelligence and practical intuition, and are now hoping to explain through their Global Coherence Initiative the mysteries of connections between people and the earth, and even the sun.

So, we are all electric and we are all receiving and transmitting energy, each with our own personal magnetic field. Each individual cell of our 37 trillion body cells also has its own electromagnetic field and every form of life has a force within it generating an energy field from its various processes and systems. Everything has a magnetic field. Stars and planets have electromagnetic fields, and so do rocks and trees. At a microscopic level, electrons are present in all atoms, constantly revolving around the nucleus which leads to a magnetic field generated even at the atomic level.

EXERCISE 56
Feel Your Electricity

Stand comfortably with your feet shoulder-width apart.

Put your arms out straight in front of you and rub the palms of your hands firmly together, back and forward quickly for 15 seconds.

Now bring your palms very close together, but not quite touching.

What can you feel? Most likely you will feel something if you did this correctly.

This is energy. You are electric!

Now put your arms out in front again, and hold your palms upwards. Focus on your palms.

What do you feel? Some sensations? Tingling?

You are energy. It flows through you and is all around you. Everything is energy.

You are an energy communicator, constantly transmitting energy and what you contribute to your energetic field environment, like every action or movement, has consequences. The collective magnetic energy fields of all human beings across the world makes up a global energy field and it may be that the emotions you feel whether positive or negative, the energy you create and your acts of kindness, affect your field environment and affect all life as all things are interconnected by connection to the Earth's magnetic fields.

EXERCISE 57
Become More Aware of Your Life Energy

Sit somewhere quiet and where you feel comfortable and without distraction.

Close your eyes, and as you breathe deeply, be grateful for all the processes that are happening inside you, making you the unique human that you are.

Focus on becoming more aware of the electricity and life force or power that flows through you.

You have an infinite source of this electricity. You are floating in an ocean of energy that is all around.

Everything is energy.

You can dial up this power with your thoughts and from your heart at any time, lighting up your cells and radiating positive vibrations from your core.

As you think about this energy flowing within, start also thinking about others and how they are energy flowing in motion too.

Build awareness of how you and others are constantly transmitting your energy and think about the consequences of how we all vibrate.

Be grateful for being given the gift of this life energy, and be grateful for the gift of awareness.

The power of gravity

Everything on Earth is energy. Everything is moving whether visible or not, and our planet is also moving, with gravity holding it and other planets in orbit around the sun. Think about the moon; it's rotating around the Earth and the gravitational pull of the moon controls the tides of the oceans. With water making up around 70% of our body it should be no surprise that human bodies are sensitive to energy fields, movements of other planets and the gravitational pull of the moon. Gravity creates stars and planets by pulling together the material from which they are made. Einstein discovered if you shine a torch upwards, the light will grow redder as gravity pulls it. You can't see the change with your eyes, but scientists can measure it. Gravity is what holds our world together and gravity is what keeps you on the ground and what makes things fall. Earth's gravity comes from its mass which makes a combined gravitational pull on all the mass in your body and that's what gives you weight. If you were on a planet with less mass than Earth, you would weigh less than you do here.

Our fast spinning planet

Do you ever think about how fast the planet you are living on is moving? We are all on board this constantly, fast-moving planet, although like sitting on a plane when it is flying through the sky, we likely don't notice that the thing we are on is moving at all. It's easy to believe that we are, for example, standing still, when we are, in fact, moving, with gravity holding us tightly to the surface of this planet. We move with the Earth and don't notice its rotation but it is spinning on its axis once every day. If you were standing on the equator you will be moving with the Earth at approximately 1000 miles an hour. This speed gets less as you move away from the equator but wherever we are, gravity holds us tight to this fast spinning planet and we don't notice its rotation.

The difference in effective speeds causes great wheels of water and air to circulate. The Gulf Stream, for example, which carries warm water from the Gulf of Mexico towards the UK, making our weather warmer and wetter than it otherwise would be, is part of a giant wheel of water in the North Atlantic Ocean that contains more water than all the rivers of the world put together. It circulates and moves because of the energy of our turning planet spinning on its axis, and revolving around the sun.

We are about 150 million km from the sun and at that distance it takes us 365 days to make a loop around. However, the sun is only one star and there are many islands of stars in our galaxy which all are moving. The galaxy itself, of which all these stars are part, is also constantly spinning at great speed.

The universe is an expanding energy

The Earth is anchored to the sun by gravity and follows along at the same fast speed, and the Milky Way moves in space relative to other galaxies. It is moving as are all the other galaxies, and they are all moving away from each other as the universe expands. The galaxies aren't moving through space, they're moving in space, because space is also moving. The universe has no centre and everything is moving away from everything else as was first shown by Hubble in 1925. The universe could therefore be thought of as infinite, and although there are different schools of thought on this, there is agreement that it's expanding away from everything else. It is an expanding energy.

Initially, Earth was believed to be the centre of the universe, which consisted only of those planets visible with the naked eye and an outlying sphere of fixed stars, but by the twentieth century, observations of spiral nebulae revealed that our galaxy is one of billions in an expanding universe grouped into clusters and superclusters. By the end of the twentieth century, the overall structure of the visible universe was becoming clearer, with superclusters forming into a vast web of filaments and voids. Superclusters, filaments and voids are the largest structures that we can properly observe at present, and at larger scales the universe becomes homogeneous. Since there is believed to be no 'centre' or 'edge' of the universe, there is therefore no particular reference point with which to plot the overall location of the Earth in the universe other than using that which we can see. Earth is therefore, by definition, only at the centre of Earth's observable universe.

Everything is in motion

This all might sound very complex and hard to comprehend, but the important point to understand is that everything in the universe is always in motion and that the universe is expanding. Humans are always moving, other forms of life are always moving, Earth is always moving, all the planets are moving, galaxies are moving and the universe is always moving, and all the movement is because of energy. Even though it may look as if you are just sitting still sometimes, you are actually not only moving a lot on the inside but also at great speed externally on the Earth, which is moving around the Sun, in the moving Milky Way, amongst other moving galaxies and through the expanding universe! All because of energy.

We know everything is moving but what about items in the universe that we think of as solid or still? What about rocks, or a chair? We know that the earth on which these objects exist is moving, but quantum physics explains that at subatomic level, these 'solid' objects are also moving.

"If quantum mechanics hasn't profoundly shocked you, you haven't understood it yet. Everything we call real is made of things that cannot be regarded as real." – Niels Bohr

Things that look solid are made up of vibrational energy fields at the quantum level and anything that exists in our universe, whether seen or unseen, broken down into and analysed in its purest and most basic form, consists of pure energy or light which resonates and exists as a vibratory frequency or pattern. Solid matter as we conventionally understand it does not exist as all the particles that make it are merely vibrations of energy. A table may look solid and motionless, but within the table are millions of millions of subatomic particles running around and bouncing with energy. At the atomic, subatomic and quantum levels, the table is pure energy that vibrates. Everything is energy and energy vibrates.

Nothing disappears, it just changes form

Where does this energy come from? Whatever you believe about the ultimate origins of energy, it may be helpful to accept that we just don't know for sure, and that this is the beautiful unknown of being alive. Have faith however, that whatever created you knows more than you ever can in this lifetime and that you are here for a reason and as an invaluable part of the whole.

The energy we encounter and use every day has always been with us since the beginning of the sun and the universe, it just changes form all around us by the law of the conservation of energy. Nothing ever disappears, it just changes form and the ideas of a beginning and an end are maybe human concepts that, in terms of energy are, unhelpful.

"Everything in Life is Vibration." – Albert Einstein

We know that everything in our universe exists as a vibratory frequency or pattern. Everything is vibration. We are transmitters and receivers of energy and vibration, radiating our own unique energy signature. We are made of cells, which are made of atoms, which are made of particles, which are actually just vortices of energy, constantly spinning and vibrating uniquely and our 'vibrational fitness' is important not only to our own body, mind and spirit, but to everything in the universe.

Become more aware of your vibrations

Different parts of us have different vibrations, at different times, and this energy is always flowing and changing form. The higher the frequency of our energy or vibration, the lighter we will feel physically, emotionally and mentally. We will experience greater personal power and clarity. When we say someone is giving good vibes, they are resonating at a high frequency which feels good for them and everyone they come into contact with. High energy feels better. It is a force for good in the world. Think of compassion, love, peace and kindness; these are high vibration states and they will make you and others feel great!

When you become more aware of your vibrations and the flow of energy within and around you, you can consciously channel this and bring focus on creating the life you want. We can control our vibrational frequency to attract to us that which matches our vibration. Whatever area of your life you want to improve, you have to raise the frequency of your thoughts and emotions so you resonate with what you want. When you're sending out low frequency waves, the universe will resonate with the magnetic field those waves create, and will send them back to you, which includes them coming back from the people in your life.

It might all seem abstract and hard to comprehend if you're new to the concept of vibrational energy, but it is possible to see a physical expression of invisible energy waves or vibrations in a process called cymatics, which is effectively the science of how soundwaves affect matter. Sand is subjected to different sounds, or frequencies, and these vibrations create different geometric shapes in the sand because of the waves.

If we pass soundwaves through water, patterns in the water change and certain types of classical music have been shown to produce complex and beautiful patterns where as harsh music produces chaotic and disorganised patterns. It's no coincidence that when we hear uplifting, inspirational or calming music, it affects how we feel as the energy flow within us is changed by the vibrations of the particular music.

Colour is also a vibration like music, and when we look at a beautiful view, or a piece of art, we experience the effects of different energy waves. Think about your home or working space. Are the colours of your environment helping you feel calm, excited, uplifted, inspired? When we understand that colour is a vibration, we can enhance the spaces we control to create the vibrations we want. We can choose to spend time with art and we can also engage more with the ultimate free art gallery that is nature.

Every frequency that passes through our bodies and minds is organising the molecules of our bodies. Just like how our fingerprints are unique, so is the energy field of each person and your body, which is 70% water, is always responding to the vibrations around it.

> *"Energy moves in waves. Waves move in patterns. Patterns move in rhythms. A human being is just that, energy, waves, patterns and rhythms. Nothing more. Nothing less. A dance." – Gabrielle Roth*

Your vibrations determine what you attract

Your 'vibration' is really just a fancy way of describing your overall state of being. You may have heard of the 'law of attraction,' which describes the ability to attract into our lives whatever we are focusing on using the power of the mind to translate our thoughts into reality. If you focus on negativity you will remain in the pattern of sending and receiving negative vibrations. If you focus on positive thoughts and have inspirational goals, you will find a way to achieve them. Everything that manifests in your life is there because it matches the vibrations from your thoughts. The energy of your thoughts creates your reality so it's important to become acutely aware of your thoughts, words and feelings. The lower your vibration the more likely you are to attract circumstances that mirror this, and the higher the vibration, the more good you will attract. Like energy attracts like energy. Everything has its own vibrational frequency and when we say a person has 'bad vibes', we mean their waves are at a low level.

"Everything is energy and that's all there is to it. Match the frequency of the reality you want and you cannot help but get that reality. It cannot be any other way. This is not philosophy. This is physics." – Albert Einstein

Avoid negative vibrations

If you turn your attention to bad news and problems, you are immersing yourself in this negative energy field and your brain will be busy growing neural circuits of stress and worry. Unfortunately, we live in a society where the media is driven by bad news, but things are actually getting 'better' in many areas. For an illuminating read evidencing some of these improvements which are mostly unreported, check out Hans Rosling's excellent book, *Factfulness, Ten Reasons We're Wrong About the World – and Why Things Are Better Than You Think.*

The news features what's wrong, but there is also a lot that is right and great. If you allow others to fill your consciousness, you are at the mercy of their consciousness. Rather than being the passive recipient of outside news, choose your own edit and be a curator. If you choose to consume positive, inspirational and uplifting material, you will build neural networks created from the positive content. Audit your surroundings, who you interact with, what you watch, etc. and start to become much more aware of the vibrations you consume.

"Your frequency determines the amount of light you attract." – Anon

Your frequency introduces you

We are always communicating energetically. Before you have spoken a word, your frequency has relayed volumes of information about you and your state.

Have you ever walked into a room and thought someone seems like they're in a foul mood? You could likely feel their energy or their 'bad vibes'. You will no doubt have walked into a room and felt uplifted by the energy of someone transmitting 'good vibes'. Raising your vibration is simply a change of the frequency you are transmitting, and by changing the frequency, you'll be sending out new information. So, if you want to connect with high-energy positive people, focus on being a transmitter of high energy positive waves.

EXERCISE 58
Monitor Your Vibrations

Ask yourself at the end of any day, how have you been vibrating? How did your vibrations flow and change?

Draw a simple graph to show your vibrations throughout the day, scoring yourself on a scale of 1–10, where 10 is when you felt you were vibrating at a very high frequency and 1 for when you felt you were vibrating at a very low frequency. Draw a line across the bottom of a piece of paper, showing the time of day in hour intervals, and then draw a line up from the start of that line showing your score scale of 1–10. You can now plot how you think you were vibrating at different times of the day.

Let's call this your 'vibrational frequency graph,' and of course, it is not an exercise in trying to be exact, but rather to encourage you to become more aware of how you are vibrating.

The highest levels of vibrational frequency include love, appreciation, peace, joy, acceptance and courage, so practice being in these states.

By raising your vibration you will create a more fulfilling and connected life.

"As you think you vibrate. As you vibrate you attract." – Abraham Hicks

Expand yourself

We've discussed how the universe is expanding. To be in alignment with the universe, work on expanding yourself, becoming more and being open to possibility, rather than being closed to new experiences and being 'set in your ways', operating with rigid thinking. Step out of your comfort zone, travel, meet new people, learn new skills, open your mind to new ways of looking at things. This may be the simplest secret to feeling harmony in your life and which you control. Pursue an expanded self and operate from a high frequency as much as you can.

We experience everything with our five physical senses and everything is conveyed through vibrations. Thoughts are vibrations, emotions are vibrations, you are vibrations. We tend to learn that reality is made up of separate physical material things, and our world is an independently-existing, objective one. However, as we discussed in Step 6, the universe exists as an entanglement of interconnectedness. By using the power of your imagination, you can match your vibration to that which you desire and then all the things in your experience will gravitate to meet that. The way we direct our awareness also produces changes in the atoms and molecules of our bodies.

EXERCISE 59
Feel Your Heart Energy

As soon as you wake up in the morning put your hand on your heart and feel it beating.

Focus on the electricity it is generating and the field of electromagnetic energy radiating from you.

As you feel each beat, be grateful for your heart as a source of energy.

Think of this energy as being love and commit to letting this energy lead you.

Breathe deeply and send this love energy as positive healing intentions to someone you know is struggling in some way in life.

Be thankful for your awareness, be thankful for your energy, and be thankful for the greatest vibrational state that is love.

"Change your inner thoughts to the higher frequencies of love, harmony, kindness, peace and joy and you'll attract more of the same." – Wayne Dyer

Build awareness of your vibrational frequency. The vibration of the thoughts you have will create the life you will have, so it's smart to raise your energy to its highest vibration to get a deeper, and more fulfilling connection with the universe. You can practice raising your vibration in lots of ways, and the more you practise, the more you will unconsciously or habitually vibrate at higher frequencies.

EXERCISE 60
Practise Raising Your Vibration

There are many ways you can raise your vibrations and if you have been following the SYSO System you will likely already be living at a higher frequency much more often than you were. However, here are just a small number of examples of actions you could take to elevate your vibrational energy. These will not only make you feel better, but you will also be more fun to be around.

1. Move your body. The human body is made to move. Make sure you have scheduled lots of movement in your day in whatever form you enjoy. There are endless ways to move. You don't have to call it exercise, that's just a label, but find regular fun ways to keep physically active.

2. Sing. It doesn't matter how good you think your singing is, but singing is possibly one of the most underrated things you can do to raise your vibration. Singing releases endorphins and oxytocin, improves cognition, can lower blood pressure, tones your facial muscles, and can boost your immunity.

3. See people you love frequently and tell them how much they mean to you and how you appreciate them in your life.

4. Laugh! We know laughter is the best medicine. Laughing is an express vibration-raiser. Laughing feels good and it's contagious.

5. Volunteer and contribute.

6. Surround yourself with colours that uplift you.

7. Make your environment a happy place and clear of clutter.

8. Practise gratitude. Become more aware of all the things you love and how abundant you really are. Make notes of the things you are grateful for.

9. Foods have a vibrational energy, so eat healthily to nourish every cell in your body. Processed foods, sugar, bad fats and salt have a low vibrational energy.

10. Drink water. It is an energetic life force that cleanses and hydrates your body. We are made up of 70% water and we need to flush out toxins to keep our vibrational energy levels up.

11. Schedule quiet time to meditate and feel a sense of calm.

"Become a conscious vessel for the life force that is always flowing through you." – Christiane Northrup

Life force

Growing or dying is the nature of life, but dying is a word humans have invented to signify the end, when really energy is just transforming into something else. Nothing ever dies or is gone, it just transforms into something else. We can't explain this life force in the same way we can explain other energies. We can't prove where the life force comes from and scientists have been unable to recreate life energy except by reproduction and embryo fertilisation processes.

The best humans have come up with in explaining this animating life energy force that is in all of us, is the idea that a spirit inhabits the body and then leaves, although there is no factual explanation of how and why this happens. We simply do not know for sure, and there may also be other invisible energies that are part of this life force, but which we can't comprehend with our limited senses.

Many cultures and spiritual practices focus on the idea of this force within us, they just have different names for it. In Indian, it's called *Prana* which simply means breath in the ancient Hindu language of Sanskrit, and in Hinduism this force is believed to survive the death of the body and can return through reincarnation. In Western cultures, this life energy is referred to as the spirit, and in Hebrew, it's *Ruah*. In Japanese it's *Ki*, in Egyptian it's *Ka* and in Greek it's *Pneuma*.

The Chinese call life energy *Chi* (Qi) and believe this force contains female (yin) and male (yang) energies. It's possible to achieve perfect balance between the two opposites of yin and yang, by opening chakras so the Chi energy can flow through the body into all energy vortexes. The concept of Chi comes from the Taoist spiritual tradition, and revolves around the currents, flows and rhythms of the world, of which we are a part. The life force is believed to be the spiritual essence and force, which flows within and throughout all of existence including humans, plants, animals, Earth and the universe.

In Christianity, the life force is called the Holy Spirit which is understood as an omnipresent divine presence believed to be within the soul of each individual and which links all of life together. As in Judaism, and many other religions of the world, spiritual energy is defined as coming from the divine love of God which is eternal and constant. It's just the methods for connecting with this divine love of God which vary from one religion to the next.

The Holy Spirit, Chi and Prana are all describing the same energy principle; that invisible spiritual currents flow throughout the world, animating and connecting everything. Whichever way you choose to describe this life force, the principles are the same.

Energy healing

The body used to be thought of as a three-dimensional anatomical structure, but in more recent years, there has been a far great awareness that the body is actually a process, and constant flow of energy and information. Energy healers have known this for a long time but many conventional medical practitioners have dismissed energy healing as scientifically unproven. There is, however, now a growing body of evidence about not just the mind–body connection in healing but also on many of the specific practices that focus on how energy is flowing through our bodies. To ignore this increased understanding of energy flows and the healing properties of energy work will likely lead to a continuation in the tendency to medicate ourselves with pills and potions when something doesn't seem right with our bodies, rather than looking for natural remedies. Medicating is at epidemic levels and the problems are getting worse, so it would seem wise for society and the conventional medical profession to embrace the role of energy healing in mainstream medicine, sooner rather than later.

> *"In every culture and in every medical tradition before ours, healing was accomplished by moving energy." – Albert Szent-Györgyi*

For centuries, healers in several traditions have believed in the energetic body. In India, Japan, China, Thailand and Tibet there has long been a belief in channels of energy, or meridians, or *sens*, or *nadis* along which our vital life energy flows. Life in these traditions is considered to be a bioelectrical and vibrational energy phenomenon, and being healthy involves balancing energy. Traditional Chinese medicine is the oldest continuous medical system in history with branches including acupuncture, herbalism, massage and *qigong*, and they all use the same concept that our body has a vital energy life force, which when unbalanced or blocked, will cause us to become ill.

Even though traditional medicine hasn't been open to these less measurable energy healing practices until recently, science has understood that our bodies are electromagnetic and has measured these frequencies using for example electrocardiographs (ECGs) and magnetic resonance imagining (MRI) scanning for many years. We are an energy field and we are immersed in energy fields, from the Earth's magnetic field to the fields produced by our heart, organs and cells. Our bodies *are* energy. They have an electrical nature. You will likely have experienced an electric shock and if you cut yourself, you will feel the pain because it is electrically carried along nerves to your brain. You are an energy being.

Energy healing traditions focus on energy pathways and various studies show that these energy pathways and points conduct electricity. When we look at meridians as networks of channels for the life force, we can appreciate the intricacy and profound connection of our body at a cellular level. We are intimately connected by the elements, energetic structure and flow of energy to all life at a cellular physical level and our Earth itself is also said to have energetic pathways (ley lines) akin to meridians. Moment to moment, the energy fields are moving and changing, and they have a radical effect on our health and prosperity.

For our health and wellbeing, we need a balanced flow of energy and practices like yoga and meditation work on these subtle energy channels to balance and support the flow of energy through our bodies. It wasn't that long ago that yoga was thought of as a slightly hippy niche practice and suggestions of energy healing were usually seen as a little woo-woo, but today there is a fast-growing understanding in mainstream society of the importance of the mind, body and spirit in our overall health.

There is also a growing awareness of areas of study around the mind, matter, body and genetics, that were historically perhaps seen as academic and dry. There is much more mainstream interest in quantum physics, electromagnetism, neuroscience, neuroendocrinology, psychoneuroimmunology and epigenetics, as we increasingly appreciate that the interplay of our mind, our nervous system and our energy flow are at the core of who and what we are. To go deeper in this area of research, you can read Dawson Church's excellent books *Mind to Matter* and *The Genie in Your Genes*. Church synthesised hundreds of studies in the fields of biology, physics and psychology, and shows that the energy fields of our brains are literally creating reality. He is also a pioneer in the field of epigenetics, explaining the remarkable self-healing mechanisms now emerging at the juncture of emotion and gene expression.

Our bodies reveal disease in our energy field before it becomes evident at the level of matter, and there is a growing body of research which shows that when energy is applied with the intention of healing, it works. Studies show that energy healing is effective for both psychological conditions such as anxiety and depression and physical conditions such as pain and autoimmune disease. Energy medicine may be the new frontier in health, and energy healing, like diet, mind-management and movement should be considered a natural pillar of wellbeing.

Think of anxiety, frustration and anger. All of these experienced states are when our thoughts and energy cause a disrupted flow in our living system, for example, when our brain patterns are out of sync with our heart. Energy builds and affects matter, and when we start with energy, we are starting with the cause of illness rather than the effects, and in doing so we can be in a much better position to manage health problems.

There are many types of energy healing, and covering them all is far beyond the scope of this book, but I will explain some of the most widespread. Many are similar but with different labels. Some focus primarily on the body physically, some on the mind, some on the spirit, some on energy meridians, and some on vibrations, although there is much crossover, and increasingly, integration of various methods.

Direct body work focuses on physical touch and alignment. Mental techniques start with thought patterns, particularly limiting or destructive ones. Spirit work usually involves flow and balance, encouraging relaxation to allow the spirit to do the work. Meridian work focuses on what are believed to be our energy lines, which can get blocked through stress, emotional trauma and poor lifestyle choices. The aim is to release the blockages so you have more life force energy flowing naturally through you. Energy healing that works through vibration is based on someone's energetic frequency and restoring the body using vibration techniques.

Being aware of the many different energy healing practices builds your awareness of resources available beyond conventional medicine and you can choose from the menu of offerings. It may be there is something in all of these approaches, and while they are all different, the underlying principle of addressing energy is the same throughout.

Tai chi is an ancient Chinese martial arts form that helps with fitness by making slow, graceful movements to encourage energy to flow easily. I start with this example as my 86-year-old mother is an active participant and enthuses about its benefits. The energy flows through the body, mending and soothing nerves and organs and helping with stress reduction, improved muscular strength, flexibility and better hand-eye coordination. Tai Chi is also perhaps the only martial art that is also foremost a meditation tool.

Acupuncture has long been practiced in the Eastern world, and the Chinese book *The Yellow Emperor's Classic of Internal Medicine* identified meridians and acupoints over 2000 years ago. More recently, acupuncture is gaining credibility in Western societies too. It involves thin, sterile needles being inserted into pressure points in the body, helping the Qi to be released. The acupuncture points are along the meridian lines in the body and this helps to relieve pain and balance the yin and yang energy to bring various health benefits.

Acupressure is derived from acupuncture and is where hands, elbows and various devices are used to heal aches and pains. Physical pressure is applied to the reflex points that stimulate the energy, enabling its free flow.

Aromatherapy uses the fragrance of oils extracted from natural ingredients to improve immunity and balance hormones.

Reiki is a cornerstone of energy healing perfected in Japan in the 1800s. In Reiki, energetic symbols are used and universal energy is channelled by means of gentle touch which activates the natural healing processes of the body to restore physical and emotional wellbeing.

Ayurvedic medicine focuses on a holistic approach to healing the body, and has been practiced in India for at least 5000 years. It is believed that humans have three basic energy types (doshas): vata, pitta and kapha. One of these is usually the most dominant, and keeping them in balance provides good health and wellbeing, through herbal treatments, breathing exercises, yoga, rubbing the skin with oils, detoxification and mantras.

Polarity therapy is a holistic approach that combines communication, listening, touch, nutrition, lifestyle and exercise to create positive changes.

Feng shui – which means 'wind and water' – is an ancient Chinese art form that balances the energies present in the air around you by moving certain items in your home such as furniture positioning, or sleeping in a certain direction to support better life outcomes.

Physical touch and massage come in many forms where touching and rubbing the body are intended to help manage and direct energy flows, release toxins and alleviate stress. Lymph nodes are powerhouses of the body, regulating fats and removing white blood cells to heal and release toxins, and a good lymphatic massage and drainage can help to improve blood circulation and remove water retention.

In **reflexology**, it's believed the hands and feet have neural pathways to all of the systems in our bodies and touching certain reflex points on the feet can, amongst many other things, stimulate the digestive system, balance hormones or reduce issues such as headaches.

When it comes to the mind, **hypnosis** can help people discard negative thought patterns stored deep in their unconscious and there is much documented success reported on how hypnotherapy has helped people quit smoking, lose weight and alter their lifestyles through communication while in deep relaxing states. Past life regression is an example of one specific technique that helps people to resolve their past life traumas by relaxing and quieting their mind, with the therapist taking them back to their past life through hypnosis.

Havening Technique is a psychosensory therapy becoming more popular, which is used to overcome past traumatic encoding using recall, touch and distraction, aiming to replace traumatic events in the person's memory to stop them being reactivated.

Meditation is one of the most widely practiced and accepted techniques to tap into our spiritual energy, and many believe meditation can create transformation and even lead to enlightenment, as well as improved focus, relaxation, stress reduction and performance, by the channelling of energy more effectively. Concentrating on your breath, or focusing on a single object like a candle, can help encourage deep meditative states. There are many different types of meditation, and although the techniques may differ, their goal is essentially the same; to quieten the mind and be an observer or witness to our thoughts.

Exercise and meditative practices help to balance the energy within the body and enlighten the mind. Walking meditation is found in many religions – it is simply walking while meditating, and running can also be considered meditating while moving. Running or cycling or walking, while connecting with nature, can be a beautiful and effective mind-management exercise.

Most religions have some form of **prayer** which provides a direct connection to spiritual energy and practitioners believe that through their praying, enlightenment can be achieved. The Native Americans and many Inuit peoples undertake a **vision quest** that includes fasting and not sleeping; a rite of passage that is designed to establish a connection with spirits.

EXERCISE 61
Channel Healing Energy

Find somewhere comfortable and quiet where you can stand without distraction.

Loosen your shoulders and body and stand with your feet comfortably apart. Inhale deeply for five seconds, followed by a long exhale of at least six seconds.

Do this four or five times, feeling the ground firmly supporting your feet and body.

Now imagine an invigorating force of powerful healing energy, coming down from above into your head and through your body, before going out through your feet, and then carrying on down to the very core of the Earth.

Breathe deeply in a rhythm that feels comfortable, feeling your feet perfectly supported by the Earth beneath you, and then imagine this electricity or life force of pure energy running from the core of the earth back up through you, healing every cell in your body, before passing back out through your head.

Do this quickly several times until you feel you have found a pace that you like.

See this refreshing energetic healing force moving into you, down through your body, out to the Earth's core, back into you, through you and out to the universe.

When you've found your rhythm, at the end of the process start to direct this healing energy as it leaves your body through the top of your head, to others, to close friends, family or anywhere you choose.

Focus on your breathing, focus on the healing energy moving through you, and feel grateful for this life force that is always available to you.

Other spiritual energy healing practices include **angel healing**, which is based on invoking archangels to facilitate spiritual and energetic healing. This can be done with the use of cards and/or with hands-on healing. Archangel Raphael is the most commonly used, and his name in Hebrew means 'healing doctor'. Angel healing is believed to cleanse and clear away blockages in the energy system.

Pranic healing works on energy which is cleansed and energised, to accelerate healing.

Shamanism and Indigenous healing were used by the Native American Indians, Australian Aborigines, and Tibetan energy healers, amongst others, to promote health and wellbeing by connecting with nature. Some shamanic and indigenous healing techniques include transpersonal dream work, meditation, rites of passage, pilgrimages to sacred places and medicinal herbs.

Moxibustion is an ancient Chinese practice that helps to regulate the flow of Qi in the body using a herb called moxa which would be burnt and placed near different pressure points on the body to help release the blocked energy.

Most religions and cultures have a ceremony or practice that they believe can deliver healing through the receiving of spiritual energy, such as the **Laying on of Hands** in Christianity, which is a form of healing that transfers the spiritual healing energy of God through the conduit (the person laying hands on the sick) to the sick individual. Many also anoint the sick with oil as depicted in the Bible.

Emotional freedom technique (EFT) releases trapped emotions or stubborn thoughts by tapping acupoints along the body's meridians while repeating statements regarding the issue. It helps to release pent-up emotions and aids the free flow of energy, enabling the body to maintain balance. EFT is often called tapping.

Vibrational medicine is based on the principle that, in essence, all creatures are made up of cells vibrating at a certain frequency, and every thought and emotion we have can be measured as a frequency. Vibrational medicine facilitates healing by introducing a new, healthier frequency to offset the negative vibration. One of the easiest ways to introduce positive vibrations is through colour, sound or the elements. Walking barefoot on the earth or carrying a rose quartz crystal can raise your vibration. After thousands of years of growth and refinement, **crystals** have been found to be some of the highest frequency objects we have and by laying crystal grids on strategic energetic points on your body, their high frequencies can balance emotional issues, physical pain and your energy flow.

Using sound vibrations can change the state of the mind from a conscious waking state to a deep and relaxed state. It's said that a **sound healing** session is the equivalent of a deep REM sleep and things such as gongs, Tibetan singing bowls and crystal singing bowls are the most popular tools used in sound healing, but tuning forks, singing and chanting are also used.

EXERCISE 62
Feel the Music in You

Sit alone somewhere comfortably.

Play some relaxing music. Focus on becoming more aware of the flow of energy in the form of soundwaves that you are receiving.

Think about the different energy waves of different pieces of music and imagine how these waves are flowing to you and through you.

Remind yourself that most (around 70%) of your body is water and as you listen to the music, feel the energy waves flowing through the water that you're made of.

Just relax and feel what you feel.

Bringing awareness to the soundwaves can bring a deep sense of calmness to your ocean of emotion.

"Music can heal the wounds that medicine cannot touch." – Debasish Mridha

One area of energy work that is increasingly being incorporated into mainstream wellbeing is **breath work**, and we have looked at this already in some of the exercises, particularly in Step 3 Exercises 29 and 30. Breath work just refers to any type of breathing exercises or techniques designed to improve energy flow and health. We know how important breathing is in exercise, meditation and yoga, where you intentionally change your breathing pattern to change how you feel, which works by oxygenating the body and increasing blood flow. Studies reveal that, by changing the patterns of breathing, it is possible to reduce stress, relieve symptoms of anxiety, improve physical health and endurance. Rapid and deep breathing leads us to release more carbon dioxide from the body than usual, causing the blood to become more alkaline and retain more oxygen.

Whether you practice formal breath work or not, building awareness of how you are breathing and understanding the physiological changes breathing differently can cause is very important for personal development and self-management.

EXERCISE 63
Practise Box Breathing

Sit upright, with your feet flat on the floor.

Slowly and deeply inhale through your nose counting to four.

After four seconds of deep inhaling, your lungs have now filled with air. Hold this breath for another slow count of four.

Then exhale through your mouth for four more beats.

Finally hold your breath counting to four.

Repeat this process several times and become aware of how you are in control of your breathing and how changing how you breathe can change how you feel.

This practice of four deep breaths in, holding for four, exhaling for four and holding for four, has been called 'square', or 'box', breathing and it can be done discreetly anytime to calm your nervous system and bring focus.

In many ways it is the opposite of panic attack breathing, where panicked breaths are reactive, short and from the chest.

Chakras

In energy healing, there is a focus on chakras, which are believed to be energetic points in our body. There are seven chakras, with each being associated with a particular body part, and when all seven chakras are aligned, a person feels in 'full flow'. However, if one chakra is blocked by negative energy or is too open, aches and pains can be felt in that area or there may be emotional issues. The Sanskrit word *chakra* literally translates as wheel or disk, and in energy work it refers to wheels of energy throughout the body, starting from the base of the spine through to the crown of the head.

Activating chakras to balance spiritual energy is often the goal of various healing techniques, and many ancient writings refer to these 'vortexes' in the body where the chi flows. When all seven main chakras are open, the person's chi can flow up and out of the crown chakra to connect with the spiritual energy. Since everything is moving, it's essential that our seven main chakras stay open, aligned and fluid. If there is a blockage, energy cannot flow. Yoga is intended to realign the body through various held physical positions (asanas) and these poses encourage the mind, body and soul to work together with the result of beneficial chi energy flowing freely through the chakras.

Located at the base of the spine and extending through the legs to your feet, is the root chakra symbolising your foundation and connection to earth. In the lower abdomen below the navel, the sacral chakra represents your passion and pleasure and in the upper abdomen, the solar plexus chakra represents your source of personal power and confidence. In the centre of the chest, the heart chakra forms your connections with other beings, and your ability to show compassion and respect, and in the region of the neck and shoulders, the throat chakra represents accepting your originality and expressing your authentic voice. Between the brows, the third eye chakra symbolises your connection to wisdom and insight and at the crown of the head, the crown chakra represents your connection to the universe and everyone around you.

"Future medicine will be the medicine of frequencies." – Albert Einstein

Tuning into the energies of the universe

Tuning into your inner life force and being receptive to the subtle energies of the universe is at the core of all energy practices. Many of these treatments, which have been traditionally thought of as 'complementary' or 'alternative', are increasingly being considered in mainstream medicine, especially as there is fast-growing resistance to the use of medications and chemicals to treat what we consider illness today. If we are energy processes, then healing how our energy is flowing or vibrating would seem a smart place to start. We know that raising our vibrations is something we can also do at any time; not only are you healing yourself when you raise your vibes, you are helping to heal others who feel your vibration.

If energy work is new to you, keep an open mind and be aware that there is so much as humans we don't know. There are many energy healing practices. Try some of the methods if you haven't experienced them before. Find a local practitioner if you need one and as a minimum, incorporate meditation and movement into your routine. Build awareness of the energy flow and find practices that work for you.

Lead with your heart

No matter what you believe about energy healing, the SYSO System advocates any practice that leads with the heart and with an understanding that we are all energy. The heart is at the very core of who and what we are, and it does much more than pump blood. The key to living in flow involves tuning in to this centre of who and what you are, to the source of love that made you, and letting your heart lead and your energy flow freely at high vibrations. As more people lead their lives from their heart, creating heart-centred states, there will be more peace and experience of love and fulfilment in the world.

EXERCISE 64
Appreciate Energy and Your Senses

Sit comfortably and in a relaxed state without distractions.

Put your hand on your heart and be grateful for this amazing gift that beats around 100,000 times a day without you having to consciously do anything.

Now focus on your breathing. Take deep breaths in and long, slow breaths out.

After four or five breaths, start imagining this breathing coming from your heart, as if your heart is breathing as you did in Exercise 30.

Each deep breath in goes deeply into your heart, and each deep exhale out from your heart.

As you do this heart breathing exercise, start to think about the gift of your senses which enable you to process the richness of life. You focussed already on being aware of your senses right back in Exercise 2, but this time it is particularly about being grateful for them.

Think about the energy of your vision, if you are fortunate enough to have sight, and be grateful for being able to see the beauty of the world around you.

Think about your hearing, your sense of smell, your sense of taste and your sense of touch.

Not everyone has all these senses, but we all have some and they are energetic processes we can take for granted. Each is a gift we should be more consciously grateful for.

Breathe deeply and give thanks for these senses you have, and for the force of life that ignites every cell in your body.

All the 37 trillion cells that make our body are mini living systems and they all vibrate. The higher the vibration, the healthier the cells. Disease, sickness and negative thinking make our cells vibrate at a lower level, while love, happiness, laughter, compassion, gratitude and positive thinking make our cells vibrate at a higher frequency. It isn't that complicated. High vibrations in all areas of your life will make you feel better and your life will be improved with more fulfilling relationships, more joy, more clarity, more focus, more gratitude, more love and better decision-making.

"The vibration of appreciation is the closest vibration that can be experienced by a human being to that of their non-physical core energy." – Abraham Hicks

Be the creator of your life experience

Start making habits that build awareness of the energy that is you, and that is everything, and the power of this energy when directed. Consciously directing energy and attention to a new future, manifesting the life you want, is limited only by your ability to imagine it. When you tune into this, synchronicities, coincidences and new opportunities will appear in your life and you will start to become more aware of what you have been doing; you will no longer be the victim in your life, but rather the creator. Victim or creator? The choice is yours and you now have the understanding and tools to create a wonderful life of joy and usefulment. By seeing the world differently and knowing that you are not a passive recipient, you create your life reality moment by moment. The energy fields of your brain are literally creating reality.

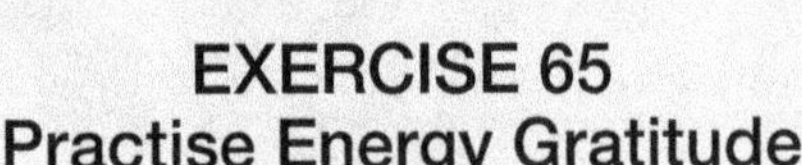

EXERCISE 65
Practise Energy Gratitude

Just pause for a moment.

Bring your focus again to feeling your heartbeat, and to its energy.

Then bring the focus to your breath, and all the energy running through you.

This is your life force and this is a gift you were given by something greater than you.

Life wanted you to be. You are loved and you are also a source of love.

Feel this energy, and feel the power of this love that created you.

Be grateful for this moment, this day and all of life, and commit to being useful, and having fun, aligning fully with your life purpose.

Practice this regularly. It doesn't take long and you can do it anywhere. Make it a habit!

The first Step of the SYSO System is to become more aware and as you have journeyed through the other six Steps in this book you will have continued to expand your level of self-awareness, harnessing more of your unlimited potential. When awareness is contracted, the flow of energy and information through your body, mind and soul is restricted. You can get caught up in toxic thinking like regret, resentment and self-pity and it's easy to succumb to unhealthy habits like overeating, lack of physical activity and negative mental processing. However, when you expand your awareness, your energy flows freely, you feel more balanced, at ease and creative, and you view yourself and the world with more understanding and compassion. You have healthy habits, more energy, are open to new possibilities for growth, and you have all the power you need to create an outstanding, joyful, passionate, fun and useful life. You are the architect of your life, you decide on your experience and you can always choose how you want to feel. Everything you need is within you right here, right now. All you had to do was sort your shit out!

"It is your road. Others may walk it with you,
but no one can walk it for you" – Rumi

Summary and Next Steps

"Your life will be no better than the plans you make and the action you take. You are the architect and builder of your own life, fortune and destiny." – Alfred A. Montapert

Congratulations! If you have read this far, you will understand that sorting yourself out isn't that complicated, you just need to know what to do and how to do it, and then you need to do the doing.
If you have followed the 7 Steps of the SYSO System, you are:

Step 1: Building your **awareness**
Step 2: Being a great manager of your **mind**
Step 3: Taking charge of your **emotions**
Step 4: Meeting your human **needs** in healthy ways
Step 5: Thinking clearly about the **purpose** of your life
Step 6: Understanding that everything is **interconnected**
Step 7: Raising your **vibrations** to make your life more fun and to enhance the lives of others.

You have lightened up, and are leading with your heart not your ego, being focused on feeling fulfilled by being useful and having fun. By following the 7 Steps, you have changed the filter through which you experience life and by changing the filter, everything looks different. You have a new perspective, clarity of purpose and excitement about the amazing adventure that is your life.

Like any learning, there will be moments of great progress and flow, and other times when it may feel challenging. Improvement seldom happens in a straight line, but when you start to see how far you have evolved, and experience how differently you feel, you can be proud of your growth, grateful for the lessons so far and excited about the future.

You can go back to any or all of the 7 Steps at any time, and the 70 exercises in this book give you plenty of opportunities to practise. Repetition really is the mother of all learning and the foundations will become more deeply embedded in your unconscious mind. The practise never stops, the growing possibilities are limitless, and the rewards of becoming more and living a joyful and fulfilling life will benefit not just you but the whole universe. Thank you! Your growth and happiness is a gift to all of us.

Wherever you are on your life journey, you now have the foundations to create the future you want and the next step is to make a clear action plan for specific areas of your life. Like setting the satellite navigation in your car, you need to know clearly and precisely where you are now, where you want to go to, why you want to go there and then start heading in that direction. These are the four big planning questions that should be in your mind at all times to inform your action plan.

Your journey is unique and only you can decide where you really want to go; you have to set your destination. When you have this clarity, you will live more effortlessly and intentionally, knowing exactly where you are going and why, which will make the journey a lot more fun.

EXERCISE 66
Four Planning Questions

Write down the following four questions and keep these always to hand as you create your action plan. They will help focus your thinking and give your plan structure and clarity.

1. Where are you?

2. Where do you want to go?

3. Why do you want to go there?

4. How are you going to get there?

These are the big simple overriding questions that should inform your action plan and we will now look at how to approach answering them.

1. Where are you? The first step is to take an audit of your current position. Directions to where you want to go depend on where you are starting from. So, start with an assessment of your life as it is right now. The clearer and more honest you are about where you are now, the more efficient your journey planning will be.

You can create a dashboard – like on a car – to bring focus to, and awareness of, the areas of your life which make up your overall experience. You can classify these in many different ways but these seven core areas are a good place to start:

1. Body and vitality
2. Emotions and meaning
3. Time
4. Relationships
5. Finances
6. Work and purpose
7. Spirituality

How are you doing in each of these areas? If you want to manage something you have to be able to measure it and if we want to measure it we have to use numbers, so the next step is to think about each area of your life and assign it a number that represents how well you're currently doing.

EXERCISE 67
Create Your Life Dashboard

Draw seven large circles of approximately equal size across a piece of paper, in landscape format. Let's call this your Life Dashboard.

Label each circle with one of the seven different areas:

Body/vitality, emotions and meaning, time, relationships, finances, work/purpose and spirituality.

Now, put a score between 1 and 10 in each circle for how you think you are currently doing in that particular area, where 1 is 'dire, it couldn't be much worse', and 10 is 'absolutely incredible, I'm crushing it'. Don't overanalyse, just write down the number which intuitively feels like an accurate assessment of where you are now in that area of your life.

Once you have done this for all seven areas, look across your dashboard and see which areas need the most attention. Usually lifting one of your weakest areas will elevate the others.

Creating and constantly assessing your performance on your Life Dashboard is one of the most important personal development tools you can use. Not only does it bring awareness and focus but you'll feel great satisfaction when you look back as you grow.

Be truthful! The truth will set you free. Only real honesty with yourself is going to help you get to where you can. There's no point in scoring your body and vitality as an 8 when you know it's a 4. What's important is how you're going to improve in the areas you choose. It isn't where you have been that matters, but rather where you are going. Even if you score yourself a 9 in all areas, there is still unlimited scope for improvement as growing and developing never stops and like the universe, we always have the capacity to expand.

When you have completed your dashboard, you have the coordinates of where you are now, and you can use these to propel yourself forward. Don't think about anyone else's dashboard. The only comparison to make is against your previous self and your previous dashboard. Your dashboard is an invaluable tool so keep it somewhere you can refer to it easily. You will be able to look back in the future, celebrate your progress and feel proud of how far you have come.

2. Where do you want to go? Most people don't really know where they are going, and only have vague goals like wanting to be happier and healthier, making more money, travelling somewhere and having better relationships, but vagueness like this is the thief of success. Clarity is your power and clarity precedes success. The clearer you are about exactly what you want, the more your brain will work out how to get there. We know from Step 2 that once you set clear goals, your unconscious mind then has a target to work towards and it works best when given direction. Make your goals clear, specific and measurable and your unconscious mind will work in its best way possible. The classic acronym SMART is a useful guide; **S**pecific, **M**easurable, **A**chievable, **R**elevant and **T**ime Sensitive. SMART goals give you clarity and a deadline for achieving them.

By being specific, your goal is clearly defined. "I want to make more money" is vague. "I want to make £10,000 per month" is specific and measurable. By quantifying your goal, you will know when you have achieved it. It's good to set goals that make you stretch and challenge yourself, but they should also be realistic. Don't stop dreaming and always think big, but by saying you'll make £1 billion in the first three months of a new business, is setting yourself up for failure. Your goals should also fit with your ultimate life purpose by being relevant, and set yourself a deadline so it doesn't become a 'sometime' in the future.

Most people's goals are not specific or clear enough and that's a little like trying to programme your satellite navigation with the loose goal of just 'going on a nice drive with good views, avoiding roadworks'. Unless you know where you're going, you will feel a little lost. If you don't know what you want in life, it's not possible to be focused and efficient with your actions.

Make goals in the specific areas from your dashboard, deciding precisely where you want to be and by what date, and ask yourself if the goals are congruent with your overall life purpose. Every goal should feed in some way into, and be aligned with, your purpose for being here.

EXERCISE 68
Write Your Own Obituary

Imagine it is the end of your life and you are writing your own obituary.

This exercise is most effective if you actually write this down so you can read it and reflect.

What is your legacy? What has been the impact of your life?

How is life better because of what you did or said, or your influence, and how?

How useful was your life?

How much did you enjoy the journey?

Feel grateful for the gift of life, for the experiences you had and feel proud and satisfied of the value your life was to other life.

By starting with the end in mind, this exercise can help bring more clarity to the goals you set now and perhaps also make you feel some extra gratitude as you realise it isn't the end of your life!

When you create clear goals, write them down. This will make them more real and 'what you write you invite!' Set goals and milestones for six months, one year, three years and five years. Make a vision board for where your life will be in five years. You know the power of visualising from Steps 2 and 3 and that your mind doesn't know the difference between real and imagined, so imagine your goals as if you have already achieved them. Seeing and feeling these as already realised is the greatest instruction you are giving your unconscious mind. Everything is created first in the mind, so make sure you are creating clearly.

3. Why do you want to go there? You may know clearly what you want, but you also need to know clearly why you want it. Your 'why' is your fuel. When things get tough, or you feel like giving up on any goal, your 'why' is the power that will drive you forward.

For each goal, you need to know clearly your reasons. If your goal is to make more money (being specific about how much and when), then ask; "why do I want more money?" It may seem obvious and you might answer with something like; "so I can do more", but keep asking why and make sure your answer leads in some way to feeding your overall purpose. The more clarity you have around your goals and how they fit with your life mission, the more likely you will be to achieve them. If you start with the end in mind, all your steps should take you in that direction.

EXERCISE 69
Know Your Why

Pick three of what you consider to be your most important goals. You should do this exercise for all your goals, but let's just focus on what you consider to be your top three initially.

On a piece of paper create three evenly spaced columns and in the left column write the three goals you have selected. These can be from any areas of your dashboard.

In the next column write your reasons for wanting to achieve each of these goals. The process of writing will help focus your thinking on the real underlying 'whys' that drive what you do.

In the final column write down how each of these goals fits with your overall life purpose.

You may not be used to examining the reasons that lie behind your choice of goals, but making this approach a habit will help make sure your goals are not only aligned with your life purpose, but also that you have the best 'fuel' to drive you towards them.

You can now examine all your goals and refine what is really important to you.

By encouraging you to think about your reasons, or the 'why' behind everything you do, this should help you live more efficiently and effectively, aligned with your biggest why; your life purpose which is your guiding star.

4. How are going to get there? Now you know where you are, and have a clear vision of where you want to be, and why, you just need an action plan of what you are going to do to get there. For each of your goals, starting with the one that needs most attention, focus on the steps you will take to get there. Understanding and planning is good, but *action* is what will get you the life you want. If I would like a cold beer from the fridge, I can talk about where I am now and what I would like, and theorise all I want about strategies to get one, but I have to take action, get off my backside and go to the fridge to get the beer. I could actually ask someone else to get it for me, of course, and that's fine too but it still involves taking action and having influence.

Taking action against clearly defined goals is the key to your progress. It isn't different from any desired outcome, whether it's getting a beer from the fridge, making a million or running a marathon. When you know your outcome and where you are now, you can make a clear plan and then you must take action. The distance between anything you want and making it reality is action.

"The path to success is to take massive determined action." – Tony Robbins

Now you can look at the various areas of your life and create a clear action plan for each. If you aren't taking action and moving in the direction of your goals, you need to work out what's stopping you. There could be practical reasons that just need a revised plan but often the blocks we have to creating the life we want are internal barriers we make inside ourselves. These could be our beliefs, conflicts in our values or because we haven't learnt how to think effectively and create action-activating thought patterns. The tools you need to eliminate most of these potential internal blocks are in Steps 2 and 3, and as you have developed your awareness, you'll be able to spot these blocks early and make sure you focus on action and follow through.

A big reason people stumble is they haven't got an effective thinking technique in place when it comes to the moment of deciding whether to take action or not. As well as having a clear strong 'why' for fuel, you also need to practice self-discipline and make it a habit not to negotiate with yourself.

Remember, your mind works for *you*. If your plan is to exercise today but you are questioning whether to go, you need to check in on your self-discipline habits. You know it is smart to go, you know it will make you feel good and you know it is part of your plan. So, don't negotiate with yourself, don't engage in an internal debate, just focus on your why and what it will feel like to have exercised and then just go. The hardest part is getting out of the door. As Jim Rohn said, "You either pay the price of discipline or the price of regret", and as soon as you decide and take action you will already be feeling good that you did.

Making smart habitual 'go' decisions at these important action junctions is one of the most important techniques for achieving your goals. The more you make clear action-activating decisions like this, the better you will feel about yourself, which will make you want to make *more* action-activating decisions. You can't bullshit yourself. Impressing yourself is a key part of building self-confidence and success and a great way to impress yourself is to take action when you know there was a choice not to.

As you now create your own clear and focused personal action plan, to take your life and your fulfilment to a whole new level, it is useful to keep a checklist of the 7 Steps of the SYSO System at hand. The Steps don't go out of date, they are applicable all the way through your life and are a distillation of what many of the most fulfilled people have known for a long time; life isn't that complicated unless you choose it to be.

EXERCISE 70
The SYSO System Checklist

Keep to hand the 7 Steps or principles of the SYSO System. Write them down somewhere always easily accessible, on paper or on your phone, a notice board at your desk or on your computer.

Regularly check in with yourself to see how you are doing by asking these seven questions at any time:

Am I becoming more **aware**?

Am I managing my **mind** to work for me?

How well am I taking charge of my **emotions**?

Am I meeting my **needs** in healthy ways and am I clear about the priorities?

Do I know clearly the **purpose** of my life?

Do I appreciate the **interconnectedness** of life?

How am I raising my **vibrations**?

The quality of your life is largely determined by the questions you ask, and by asking these questions regularly you will automatically embed the 7 Steps of the SYSO System into your unconscious operating system.

If you have read this book and taken the action suggested, your life will already be very different to when you started. You are in the driving seat, you are taking responsibility for your experience and you understand the invaluable role you play.

Everything you need to create an amazing life is already within you and you don't need to wait for anyone to light your fire. You have your own matches and you now know how to use them. Light up, enjoy your life and shine on those you meet on your journey. You never know what others are trying to sort out in their own lives. Kindness is your love shining through. And once you've sorted your own shit out, life is a lot more fun and you become a greater gift to those around you. Your impact never stops.

"Those who are happiest are those who do the most for others." – Booker T. Washington

NOTES

NOTES

NOTES

NOTES

NOTES

NOTES

NOTES

NOTES

NOTES